The **Politically Incorrect Guide**™ to

CAPITALISM

The Politically Incorrect Guide™ to
CAPITALISM

✳ ✳ ✳ ✳ ✳ ✳ ✳ ✳ ✳

Robert P. Murphy, Ph.D.

Since 1947
REGNERY
PUBLISHING, INC.
An Eagle Publishing Company • Washington, DC

Library of Congress Cataloging-in-Publication Data
   Murphy, Robert P., (Robert Patrick), 1976–
   The politically incorrect guide to capitalism / Robert P. Murphy.
   p. cm.
   Includes index.
   ISBN 978-1-59698-504-9
   1. Capitalism—United States. 2. United States—Economic policy. 3. United States—Economic conditions. 4. Free enterprise. I. Title.
   HB501.M88 2007
   330.12'2—dc22

                              2007001846

Published in the United States by
Regnery Publishing, Inc.
One Massachusetts Avenue, NW
Washington, DC 20001
www.regnery.com

Distributed to the trade by
National Book Network
Lanham, MD

Manufactured in the United States of America
10 9 8 7 6 5 4 3 2 1

Books are available in quantity for promotional or premium use. Write to Director of Special Sales, Regnery Publishing, Inc., One Massachusetts Avenue NW, Washington, DC 20001, for information on discounts and terms or call (202) 216-0600.

This book is dedicated to my father,
whose subscription to the
Conservative Chronicle and daily
listening to Rush Limbaugh
got me interested in
free market capitalism.

CONTENTS

Contents

ARE YOU A CAPITALIST PIG? TAKE THE QUIZ AND FIND OUT!

1. How much should a worker be paid?

a) On a sliding scale depending on how important his work is to society.

b) Enough to support his family.

c) Just enough to keep him from quitting.

2. How much should a business charge for its products?

a) Just enough to cover expenses.

b) Enough to keep employment high in the industry.

c) The highest price it can.

3. If you are a car producer, how many deaths should your product cause per year?

a) Zero, of course!

b) Obviously, as few as possible—the goal should be to make cars the safest form of transportation.

c) Whatever number of deaths makes your firm the most money.

4. You're hiring a receptionist. One applicant is efficient and the other is gorgeous. Which should you choose?

a) The efficient one.

b) The gorgeous one.

c) Hire the gorgeous one if she attracts enough extra business to compensate for her inefficiency, otherwise hire the efficient one.

5. What's your opinion of commercials?

a) They are an insidious form of corporate brainwashing that cater to our baser instincts and prejudices.

b) They're occasionally clever, especially during the Super Bowl, but in general commercials are banal and tiresome.

c) They can be a great way to boost sales, so long as you've correctly identified your target audience.

If you answered (c) to three of the questions above, you might be a capitalist pig. And if you are, oink away, because, as we'll see, it's better—for everybody—if we have more capitalist pigs and fewer bureaucratic swine.

Chapter One

CAPITALISM, PROFITS, AND ENTREPRENEURS

hese days, everyone has an agenda. Feminists demand "equal pay for equal work." Environmentalists want to save the earth from the ravages of industry. Social scientists want to reconstruct society on "rational" grounds. Natural scientists want to promote biodiversity and develop alternative energy sources. Consumer advocacy groups want to improve product safety. Moralists decry commercialization. Luddites yearn for the simple agrarian society of the past. Beneath their differences, all these groups share one passion: they *despise* capitalism.

So what is capitalism, anyway?

Capitalism is the system in which people are free to use their private property without outside interference. That's why it's also known as the free enterprise (or free market) system, because it allows people freedom to choose: freedom to choose their own jobs, freedom to sell their products at whatever prices they like, and freedom to choose among products for the best value.

In the United States, many of us take capitalism for granted, but under a socialist government or in a tribal system, jobs are assigned by the

Guess what?

- The word "capitalism" was originally a Marxist smear.

- No economic system has ever been more successful at continuously raising standards of living than capitalism.

- Profits are proof that resources are used effectively.

authorities. In "managed" economies, prices might be set and import and export quotas might be enforced. In many socialist countries there is no right to private property at all: everything is owned—or could be confiscated—by the state for the benefit of "the people."

Laissez-faire versus regulation

Of course, the "capitalist" system of the United States is different from the "capitalist" system in, say, Norway. And, for that matter, America's capitalist system today is far different from what it was in 1900. A country can have private property and allow certain economic freedom, but also fence it in with heavy government regulation.

A Book You're Not Supposed to Read

Planned Chaos by Ludwig von Mises; Irvington-on-Hudson, NY: Foundation for Economic Education, 1947.

Most modern critics of capitalism fear freedom—they fear the results of allowing people to decide their own economic affairs and letting the unregulated market run its course. They think regulators and bureaucrats know better than private citizens making their own voluntary arrangements. To show how baseless these fears are, in this book we will examine "pure" capitalism, even though it doesn't exist in this form today.

Free to starve?

Critics of capitalism will concede, "Yes, in a market economy the workers are 'free to choose' their jobs. But," they'll add, "so what? Workers are at the mercy of employers."

But better to be at the mercy of an employer in a free market—where you have a choice, the employer has competitors, and the worst he can do is cease giving you his money—than to be at the mercy of a state bureaucrat who makes choices for you with the force of the government behind him. The political implications—not just the economic ones—of a free market versus a socialist economy are obvious, so much so these days that they are an embarrassment to enemies of the free market.

Yes, a single mother with no savings may have to put up with quite a lot from a lecherous boss for her children's sake. But if it ever gets to be too much, she can always quit. In contrast, under a socialist system, the dissatisfied citizen's only recourses are to leave the country (if that's even allowed), or to start a revolution. So which person will likely suffer more abuse—the worker under capitalism or the comrade under socialism? Are we simply to assume that powerful people in a capitalist system are evil, while powerful people in other systems are benevolent?

Mass production for the masses

A common objection to capitalism is that it exploits the poor to serve the interests of the rich. Historically, this is precisely backward. In the alleged good old days of medieval Europe (idealized by thinkers such as John Ruskin and Hilaire Belloc), the vast majority of people either toiled in the fields to which they were bound or worked at a craft heavily regulated by a guild. Meanwhile, the elite aristocracy had a virtual monopoly on luxury goods.

What a Capitalist Said

"If capitalism had never existed, any honest humanitarian should have been struggling to invent it. But when you see men struggling to evade its existence, to misrepresent its nature, and to destroy its last remnants—you may be sure that whatever their motives, love for man is not one of them."

Ayn Rand, *Capitalism: The Unknown Ideal*

This all changed after the rise of modern capitalism. Rather than trying to entice a few rich clients, the emerging big businessmen now catered to the newly empowered working class. After all, it's silly to build a factory unless you plan on having hundreds or thousands of customers. The vast expansion in production allowed more and more families the luxury of keeping their children out of the labor force. During this "horrible" transition into the capitalist era, infant mortality dropped and life expectancy rose. The average blue-collar worker under capitalism was (and is) fantastically wealthy compared to the kings of the feudal period (except perhaps in terms of per capita castles).

Central planning versus the "anarchy" of production

Aside from the "fact" that it hurts the poor, the other major objection to capitalism is that it is allegedly chaotic. After all, in a market economy no one is "in charge" of car production, and it's nobody's job to make sure that enough newborn-sized diapers get made. The apparent chaos, or unreliability, of laissez-faire capitalism seems most evident during recessions, when unemployed workers are eager for jobs and consumers are hungry for their products but the capitalist system seems to fail everyone. Wouldn't it be much more sensible to have a group of experts draw up plans (in five-year increments, perhaps) to rationally determine how resources and workers should best be deployed?

This view is flawed in two major respects. First, it is impossible for a central authority to plan an economy. New technologies (if entrepreneurs have freedom to create new technologies), changes in consumer taste (if consumers have freedom to pursue their tastes), and the innumerable variables that can affect production, distribution, and consump-

A Book You're Not Supposed to Read

How the West Grew Rich by Nathan Rosenberg; New York: Basic Books, 1986.

tion of everything from newspapers to lawn mowers on a national or international scale are simply not "manageable" in the way socialist planners like to think they are.

Second, the planning bias completely misunderstands the role of profit and loss in a market economy. Far from being arbitrary, a firm's "bottom line" indicates whether an entrepreneur is doing what makes sense: if his product is one that people want and if he is using his resources in the best possible way. The firm's costs are themselves prices, which are influenced by the bidding of other producers who have competing uses for the same resources.

Paul Samuelson, Prophet

Nobel laureate Paul Samuelson, in his tremendously popular introductory economics text, declared as late as 1989 (!) that "the Soviet economy is proof that, contrary to what many skeptics had earlier believed, a socialist command economy can function and even thrive."[1]

The free market's effects are far from arbitrary. Every time you spend three dollars on tomatoes, you are ultimately "voting" for some of the nation's scarce farmland to be reserved for tomato production. Smokers similarly "vote" for some of the land to be reserved for tobacco production. When a business has to shut down because it is no longer profitable, what that really means is that its customers valued its products less than they valued *other* products that other businesses could make with the same materials. If a business is enjoying high profits, that's the market's indication that it is using its resources more effectively than other firms.

We won the Cold War! Or did we?

In the late nineteenth and early twentieth centuries, socialists might have had some excuse for thinking that state planning made more sense than economic freedom. After all, most of them had never been to a communist country, and most academic economists thought as they did. They believed that "in principle" a group of central planners, using the

5

techniques of abstract mathematical models, could oversee an economy much more rationally and equitably than spontaneous market forces. In the first few years after the Bolshevik revolution, many of the best and brightest college professors thought the "Soviet experiment" had demonstrated that—if he were willing to liquidate or imprison a few dissenters, reactionaries, and other spoilsports—a dictatorial strongman could achieve fantastic rates of growth for his country relative to democratic and indecisive Westerners. Moreover, such a dictator would make economic life more "just" and "equal" by redistributing income from the rich to the poor.

As the years passed, the excuses for believing in socialism disappeared, but faith in socialism didn't. Nevertheless, it was undeniable that the

Wearing Their Scorn as a Badge of Honor

The term "capitalism" is actually a misnomer; "propertyism" would be much more accurate. Karl Marx used "capitalism" to suggest that under a system of private property, only the "capitalists" benefit (whereas socialism serves *all* of society). As economist and classical liberal Ludwig von Mises explains:

> The capitalist system was termed "capitalism" not by a friend of the system, but by an individual who considered it to be the worst of all historical systems, the greatest evil that had ever befallen mankind. That man was Karl Marx. Nevertheless, there is no reason to reject Marx's term, because it describes clearly the source of the great social improvements brought about by capitalism. Those improvements are the result of capital accumulation; they are based on the fact that people, as a rule, do not consume everything they have produced, that they save—and invest—a part of it.[2]

masses in the United States lived better under capitalism than the masses in the Soviet Union did under communism—and that's setting aside the more than sixty million citizens that political scientist R. J. Rummel believes the Soviet government intentionally murdered between 1917 and 1987.

A Book You're Not Supposed to Read

Capitalism and the Historians by Friedrich Hayek; Chicago: University of Chicago Press, 1954.

Still, after the fall of the Berlin Wall, socialism's defects were too obvious to overlook. Even the leaders of Communist China announced more and more pro-market reforms, bowing to the inevitable reality that capitalism is the only system that works.

With this clear-cut empirical record, surely the opinion leaders in the Western world would sing the praises of the market economy, right? Of course not. Even though the bankruptcy of socialism is manifest to everyone, the intellectual elite continue to despise capitalism. For these people, virtually every social ill can be blamed on the free market, and the solution always involves more money and power for the government.

In this book, I'll analyze some of the more popular distortions and outright lies behind this widespread hatred of capitalism. We'll see that, contrary to critics' beliefs, a system based on private property and the incentive for profit leads people to do what's best not only for themselves, but also for society as well. (Adam Smith famously dubbed this mechanism the "invisible hand.") And when government intervenes in the market, it not only tramples on freedom and individual rights, but it also often hurts the very people it presumes to help.

What a Capitalist Said

"Capitalism is at its liberating best in a non-capitalist environment. The crypto-businessman is the true revolutionary in a Communist country."

Eric Hoffer, *Reflections on the Human Condition*

Chapter Two

THE PRICE IS RIGHT
(BY DEFINITION)

 hen a street vendor doubles the price of his umbrellas on rainy days, he's making a rational response to changing circumstances. And, as we'll see in this chapter, we all benefit from his charging what he thinks the market will bear.

Prices are signals

The key thing to remember about free market capitalism is that it is a system of voluntary exchange; buyer and seller agree to an exchange because they think it is to their mutual benefit.

A market price is the balance between how eager you are to buy something and how reluctant the producer is to sell it. If something has a high price tag, it's because it's scarce; if it has a low price tag, it's because "they're a dime a dozen." In short, market prices are not arbitrary. For instance, given that a Mercedes-Benz is expensive, if you're a consumer, you'll want to make sure your other needs are taken care of before you shell out a lot of money for a luxury car. Likewise, if you're a producer, market prices tell you what goods need to be produced. So, for example, if you're an apple grower and the price of apples is 10 cents a pound, you'll know you need to either grow a lot of apples to meet the demand

Guess what?

- Big Oil's profits are fair.
- Rent control hurts the poor.
- When government regulates prices, it creates shortages.

for inexpensive fruit or diversify into a different crop that consumers consider more valuable. When the government interferes with prices, it cripples the ability of free people to make intelligent economic decisions, just as surely as if the politicians interfered with phone lines, e-mail, or other means of communication.

The big fuss over "Big Oil"

The latest clamoring for price controls concerns the "unconscionable" profits of oil companies. Many Americans were understandably shocked at the sharp rise in gasoline prices in the mid-2000s and considered the gains of the oil companies to be unfair (especially in a lackluster economy). Even though prices eventually drifted down, pundits and politicians never stopped suggesting a windfall profits tax on oil companies or even outright price controls. They justify these proposals by claiming the federal government has to protect the average car-dependent citizen from the monstrous multinational oil companies.

But we have to ask if this "explanation" really makes sense. If the spike in gas prices were due entirely to the greediness of the oil tycoons and the helplessness of the consumer, why weren't oil tycoons so greedy and drivers so dependent on gasoline when prices were lower? Chances are the greed of the oil companies and the dependence of car drivers didn't change that much between 2004 and 2005. What changed was supply and demand.

As more countries reform their institutions in a free market direction and experience strong economic growth, their demand for oil goes up. Turmoil in the Middle East—and,

A Book You're Not Supposed to Read

Rent Control: Myths and Realities— International Evidence of the Effects of Rent Control in Six Countries by Walter Block, Milton Friedman, Friedrich A. Von Hayek, Basil Kalymon, Edgar O. Olsen, eds.; Vancouver: Fraser Institute, 1981.

What a Capitalist Said

"The price of monopoly is upon every occasion the highest which can be got. The natural price, or the price of free competition, on the contrary, is the lowest which can be taken, not upon every occasion indeed, but for any considerable time altogether. The one is upon every occasion the highest which can be squeezed out of the buyers, or which, it is supposed, they will consent to give: the other is the lowest which the sellers can commonly afford to take, and at the same time continue their business."

Adam Smith, *The Wealth of Nations*

briefly, the hurricanes that devastated America's Gulf Coast—led to supply interruptions and the fear of more interruptions in the future. These factors combined in 2005 and 2006 to push up the price of oil. The price was simply a reflection of economic reality. Taxing "windfall profits" won't repair a pipeline damaged by Iraqi saboteurs. Indeed, it would have precisely the opposite effect. Why would an oil company spend millions of dollars protecting and repairing its supply chains if the government is just going to tax away its profits?

Oil companies are in business for the long term. Unlike hair stylists or hot dog vendors, the people in the oil industry make investments—in drilling and equipment and exploration and a dozen other things—that can take decades to pay off. They justify their investments by making forecasts about the future price of oil. When the prices are high, yes, the oil companies will earn high profits, because their infrastructure is already in place. But these profitable periods offset the early years of "losses" when the company pumped money into setting up an operation. If the critics truly think the oil tycoons are charging too much, then they should form their own companies, buy their own oil fields, drill their own holes in the ground, set up their own refineries, and then sell the resulting product for less than the currently "unfair" price.

Running out of gas...

While price controls might save you some money at the pump, they will cost you time and money in the form of shortages, long lines, and perhaps rationing, because it will no longer be profitable for companies to deliver gas to your local gas station. This is happening now in Iraq, where motorists have to spend hours in line to fill up their tanks, because (continuing a tradition of Saddam Hussein's) the Iraqi government enforces a ridiculously low price for gasoline as a "benefit" to its citizens.

Perhaps the best illustration of the connection between price controls and shortages was during the OPEC (Organization of Petroleum Exporting Countries) crisis of the 1970s. The OPEC countries restricted output in order to raise prices. In response, the Nixon administration enacted price controls on gasoline. The result was long lines at pumps nationwide. Rather than letting the market price allow consumers to make their own choices about how much they were willing to pay for gas, or how willing they were to rely on public transportation, the government was forced to invent arbitrary rules to ration supply, going so far as to declare that only vehicles with particular license plates could get gas on a particular day. It is important to underscore that the lines at the pump were not caused by OPEC, but rather by the Nixon administration. The moment the controls were relaxed, people could once again buy as much gasoline as they wanted, whenever they wanted.

A Book You're Not Supposed to Read

The Age of Oil: The Mythology, History, and Future of the World's Most Controversial Resource by Leonardo Maugeri; Westport, CT: Praeger, 2006.

Price controls aren't just bad when it comes to gas and oil—they're bad all the time. In fact, when applied to housing, it means that poor people get driven out of the market.

A Book You're Not Supposed to Read

Cornerstone of Liberty: Property Rights in 21st-Century America by Timothy Sandefur; Washington, DC: Cato Institute, 2006.

Rent control (or, How to destroy a neighborhood)

Some politicians still think that setting a government cap on apartment rental rates will help poor tenants. But the facts of economic life have proven these politicians wrong time and again.

The most immediate side effect, or unintended consequence, of rent control is a housing shortage. When the government makes housing artificially cheaper, it makes tenants want to rent more apartments (than they would at the higher market price) and landlords want to rent out fewer units (than they would at the higher market price). Voilà! Rent control causes an instant housing shortage.

Rent control laws cause a housing shortage in both the short and long runs. The latter case is easy to understand: if a group of investors is considering whether to buy a plot of Manhattan real estate and spend millions of dollars to erect a towering apartment complex, it certainly makes a huge difference if they are allowed to charge the market price for each unit, or if instead the government artificially caps the rental rate at an "affordable" amount. Rent control laws cripple a city's ability to handle long-term growth, because few businessmen will want to build apartments that can be rented only at below-market prices. So the growing population is largely stuck with the existing stock of housing.

In addition to this long-term effect, there is also an *immediate* reduction in available housing after the imposition of rent controls. At first this seems counterintuitive: if an apartment building with 100 units, say, has already been erected, then wouldn't rent control at least guarantee that the 100 families in the building get a break from their greedy landlord?

Not necessarily. A central tenet of economics is that people make decisions "on the margin." In this context, the principle alerts us to the possibility that the owner of a building may choose to rent out fewer units at the artificially capped price. There are all sorts of expenses and risks that an owner takes when renting an apartment, and if the government reduces the benefits (the rental payment), landlords will engage in less of the activity. This is quite obvious if we consider a "dormer," where a homeowner rents out a portion of his house to a tenant. It may be worthwhile to do this when the tenant is allowed to pay $500 per month in rent. But if the law allows the tenant to pay only $100 per month, then in all likelihood the homeowner would prefer to have no tenants and keep the bedroom as a spare for visiting relatives, or for children coming home from college, or even just for storage. So while rent control laws didn't physically eliminate the bedroom, they did effectively remove an apartment from the rental market. In other words, not only does rent control dampen the supply of *new* housing, but it also reduces the supply of *old* housing as well!

Unfortunately, the story doesn't stop there. Besides a shortage in housing, rent control has other, more insidious consequences. For not only are there fewer apartments available, but the quality of the remaining units suffers as well, because if landlords can't charge a market rate, they'll cut corners to maintain profitability—or sell the building to someone who will.

What a Capitalist Said

"It is not from the benevolence of the butcher, the brewer, or the baker, that we expect our dinner, but from their regard to their own interest.... Nobody but a beggar chuses to depend chiefly upon the benevolence of his fellow-citizens."

Adam Smith, *The Wealth of Nations*

Because rent controls encourage landlords to reduce their maintenance expenses, apartments in rent controlled areas aren't painted as often, repairs aren't made as quickly, graffiti doesn't get erased as quickly, and the washer/dryers in the basement don't get replaced when they break down. Under rent

A Book You're Not Supposed to Read

Economics in One Lesson by Henry Hazlitt; New York: Harper & Brothers, 1946.

control there are no market penalties for shoddy service, because there is a long line of potential tenants. Thus rent control does not eliminate but rather creates "slumlords" who in a market system would have to compete to attract and retain tenants.

Ironically, another consequence of rent control is that it places an extra burden on minorities, immigrants, and other "disadvantaged" groups. Because landlords can no longer rent to the highest bidder, other criteria are used to ration the supply of housing to the demand for it. The landlord might insist on a letter of reference, a pay stub from the prospective tenant's employer, evidence of a bank account, and so on. The landlord will also have an enhanced incentive to rent only to friends or "good people" who speak his language and go to his church. In order to get into certain buildings, it is not enough for the Vietnamese immigrant who just got off the boat and speaks only broken English to faithfully make his monthly payments. Under rent control, you have to "know someone" to get into the coveted buildings. Again, this is not due merely to human nature. Anybody with the cash can walk into a Best Buy and purchase a plasma-screen television. This is simply not true when it comes to rent controlled apartments, because there are more people with the cash than there are available units.

In addition to the above flaws, rent control laws utterly fail in their alleged purpose because people *still* end up paying top dollar for high-quality apartments. Given time, businessmen will always find ways to circumvent regulations. For example, a landlord may make it his policy to deal only through large brokers. (That is, someone walking up to him and announcing, "I understand that you have a vacancy in 10D since Mrs. Green died last week, and I would be happy to pay what she was paying" will be told to go talk to a broker.) The brokers, in turn, may charge several months' rent for their services in locating apartments for their clients. Out of this fee, the brokers give a cut to the landlord to reward him for his exclusionary policy. Thus rent controls foster a cartel of sorts, where the legally allowed rent is supplemented by other types of fees. In other words, if you like the OPEC cartel, you'll love the rent control cartel.

Chapter Three

LABOR PAINS

We know that supply and demand set the prices of radios and ice cream cones. But did you know that supply and demand set wages and salaries too? Your hourly wage as an employee is how much you charge for your "product"—your labor—in the very same way that the price of a hot dog is what a hot dog vendor charges for *his* wares.

Baseball players make more than teachers! Where are our priorities?

Whenever a prima donna athlete complains about his salary, we invariably read laments about America's horrible value system. Where are our priorities, when high school teachers get $40,000 to teach mathematics to the next generation, but a loudmouth egotist gets $2 million to throw a little white ball really fast?

But the free market doesn't set prices according to moral worth. Imagine if someone said, "This nation is disgusting! A copy of the Holy Bible costs only $5, but a Nintendo GameCube has a market value of sixty times that. Where are our priorities?" I think we'd all recognize that approach as a pretty absurd way to measure the moral value of the two products,

Guess what?

- Pro sports salaries are fair.
- Giving fired CEOs "golden parachutes" makes sense.
- Unions hurt workers.
- Minimum wage laws cause unemployment.

and that's why no one talks like this. But the same principle holds true for the price of labor.

Economists often illustrate this concept with the so-called water-diamond paradox, which runs like this: In terms of their value in use, water is necessary for life, whereas diamonds are a mere luxury. Yet in terms of their value in exchange, water is virtually worthless and diamonds are coveted.

Economists have a rule to explain this apparent paradox: goods are valued according to their *marginal utility*. In other words, we never choose between *all* the water in the world and *all* the diamonds in the world. (If we did, we'd obviously pick water over diamonds.) If I take your bottle of water, it's easy for you to replace. You can pull another bottle from the fridge, or drink tap water. But if I take your diamond ring, I'd better start running.

The same principle applies to the prices of various types of labor. It is certainly true that if we had to choose between *all* the high school teachers and *all* the professional baseball players, we'd value the former more highly. But this fact has no bearing whatsoever on the value of the services of *one* high school teacher versus the services of *one* pro athlete. It is fairly easy to replace any given math teacher; there are plenty of people in the population with the requisite ability to move into secondary education should a demand suddenly arise. In contrast, there are very few people who can throw a strike at ninety miles per hour even with years of training.

There's another inconsistency in arguments complaining about the salaries of pro athletes: don't the Marxists remind us that, in a just

Economics Made Simple

marginal utility: The marginal utility of a good or service is the amount of satisfaction—utility—you get when consuming one unit of it. If you're really thirsty, the marginal utility of your first glass of water is much higher than that of your third or fourth, because your thirst diminishes after the first glass.

> ## "From the folks who brought you the weekend..."
>
> The tremendous increase in human productivity (made possible by capitalist investment and innovation) has given Western workers shorter work weeks, safer job conditions, and more generous benefits than anyone has ever enjoyed. In pre-capitalist times, nobody worried about ergonomically designed tools.

society, the workers receive the "full product" of their labor? If the Chicago Bulls hire Michael Jordan and consequently earn $25 million more per year (due to higher ticket sales, increased advertising revenue, etc.), then why shouldn't Jordan be paid accordingly? To arbitrarily demand that he be paid less just means more of the value of Michael Jordan's labor goes to the fat-cat owners of the Bulls.

Even bad CEOs deserve the big bucks

More reasonable critics of the free market don't object to large compensation per se; if an innovative new executive is brought in who can slash costs and boost sales, it's completely justified for the shareholders to reward him with millions of dollars. The reason, after all, that CEOs make high salaries in the first place is that they're expected to deliver high profits. But what of the well-publicized cases of failed CEOs who run their firms into the red, yet still collect millions of dollars after being fired?

Before analyzing these admittedly strange cases, let's think about a simpler one. Suppose Philip Morris decides to develop a tobacco-free

Professional Athlete Salaries for 2005–2006

Tiger Woods	$90 million
Michael Schumacher	$58 million
Phil Mickelson	$45 million
Michael Jordan	$32 million
Kobe Bryant	$31 million
Shaquille O'Neal	$30 million*
Valentino Rossi	$30 million
Alex Rodriquez	$29 million
Carson Palmer	$28 million
David Beckham	$27 million
Tom Brady	$26 million
LeBron James	$26 million
Ronaldinho	$26 million
Derek Jeter	$25 million
Maria Sharapova	$19 million
Michelle Wie	$17 million
Serena Williams	$10 million
Annika Sorenstam	$8 million
Venus Williams	$7 million

All figures include endorsements

* O'Neal receives the highest salary in the NBA; Bryant has the edge in endorsements

Source: Forbes.com

cigarette. Naturally, such a novel product will require a huge publicity and marketing blitz for its kickoff. To this end, Philip Morris contracts for the services of an advertising agency, spending hundreds of thousands of dollars on commercials, jingles, and strategy sessions. Despite everyone's best efforts, the product flops and Philip Morris has to discontinue it after only three weeks. Finally, imagine that Philip Morris says to the ad agency, "Please give us our money back. We hired you to generate sales for our product, and you obviously failed to deliver. Since you provided us with what, in retrospect, were useless services, we shouldn't have to pay you one thin dime."

Naturally the advertising agency would laugh off this request and refer Philip Morris to the contract, which guaranteed nothing and offered no refunds in the event of a flop. But let's push the analysis one step further: Why would the agency have insisted on this type of contract in the first place? Why wouldn't they agree to be paid only in the event of a successful campaign? Don't they trust their own abilities?

Upon reflection, the answer is quite simple. The advertising business is incredibly uncertain. If agencies were restricted to being paid only a percentage of net profits from successful campaigns, they would never agree to work on risky or uncertain products (or would work on them only with the promise of a very high percentage). Given the different incentives and the relative control over the fate of the product, companies often choose to pay flat fees to ad agencies (just as they pay flat fees to assembly line workers) and shoulder the risks themselves. If the product is a hit, the company reaps the rewards; if it's a flop, the company eats the money spent on commercials and everything else.

The same principles apply when shareholders hire a chief executive officer. Unlike routine managerial work, the task of a CEO often involves bold innovation. If the steps necessary to turn a particular company around and earn millions were "obvious," the company wouldn't be in trouble in the first place. When a new CEO comes in with ambitious plans, he knows that failure is entirely possible. If the shareholders said, "We'll pay you $20 million if you succeed, but nothing if you fail," it wouldn't be a very attractive offer at all. This is because the type of person who gets picked to head a major corporation could easily make hundreds of thousands, if not millions, for certain by consulting or offering other services less glamorous than being CEO.

What a Capitalist Said

"There is no such thing as a collective brain."

Ayn Rand, *Capitalism: The Unknown Ideal*

Nobody objects when an automobile firm tells its assembly line workers, "We will pay you $50,000 (base salary plus $5,000 bonus) if our cars sell very well this year, but we will pay you only $45,000 (no bonus) if we lose money." Yet when the same is done for CEOs—with the numbers being much higher, of course, because their successes could greatly increase corporate earnings—the principle seems scandalous.

Child labor laws are unnecessary

Another typical example of economic confusion in many people's minds is the difference between correlation and causation.

For instance, because the standard of living has improved for workers at the same time that government interventions have multiplied, people tend to assume that labor unions and government regulation are the source of the improvement—in large part because labor unions and big government, and the people who cheer them on, relentlessly tell us so. But in fact, it is the triumph of capitalism that has improved living standards and working conditions—capitalists are just too busy working and investing to take a bow.

Perhaps the best example of the confusion over correlation and causation is child labor. Yes, children worked in factories in Dickensian fashion in, well, the times of Charles Dickens. Nowadays, this practice is illegal in "advanced" countries. Hence, many people conclude that the government stepped in and mercifully spared further generations of children the filth and misery of toiling as a cog in the capitalist machine.

But does this analysis really make sense? If child labor were legalized tomorrow, would you send your eight-year-old to the factories to bring home an extra $200 or so a month (after taxes)? Of course not. If a country becomes wealthy enough that it is "obvious" that young children don't need to work, then parents don't need to elect politicians to tell them this. And if a country isn't that wealthy—

> ## What a Capitalist Said
>
> "Every workman has a great quantity of his own work to dispose of beyond what he himself has occasion for; and every other workman being exactly in the same situation, he is enabled to exchange a great quantity of his own goods... for the price of a great quantity of theirs. [A]nd a general plenty diffuses itself through all the different ranks of the society."
>
> Adam Smith, *The Wealth of Nations*

as is true today in many regions of the world—then government bans simply force the children into illegal operations (such as prostitution) so their families won't starve. Governments don't create wealth simply by passing legislation; if a sole breadwinner is to support his family, he needs productivity, not laws.

A Book You're Not Supposed to Read

The Strike Threat System by William Hutt; New York: Arlington House, 1973.

There are two other minor points on the issue of child labor. First, unions were historically among those urging for restrictions on child labor, but—as we shall see below—their motives were far from benevolent. Concern for their own paychecks rather than for the poor children drove their agitation.

The second point is that the thought experiment above really didn't make sense, as you may have discovered; even if the government legalized child labor, you really couldn't send your eight-year-old to work full-time, because the government already has rights over your child's day. Namely, the government insists that you put your kid to work learning how to read, write, and calculate (and dodge bullets, in many public schools). So it's really not true, after all, that the government has spared children from toil and instead lets them romp on the playgrounds. No, the government instead buses them into mass worker-training programs and is very resentful indeed when parents try to opt out of this arrangement, as in homeschooling.

The minimum wage (or, How to create unemployment)

The clearest example of the distinction between rhetoric and reality in labor laws is the minimum wage. According to its advocates, the minimum wage has rescued thousands upon thousands of workers from destitution. Had the government not stepped in and declared a "civilized"

A Paradox of Priorities

The very same people who remind us over and over that a person's income is no measure of his or her intrinsic worth are the ones who complain the loudest over this country's "priorities" when it comes to salaries. But if we are already agreed that a person's salary has no relation to moral worth or social importance, then why is a teacher (or nurse, or firefighter, etc.) entitled to more money than a professional athlete?

floor less than which no decent person could pay another human being, capricious employers would outdo each other in a race to the bottom. The hapless low-skilled workers have no bargaining power (they have to eat, after all) and hence would be forced to accept whatever crumbs they were offered.

There are so many things wrong with this typical view that it's hard to know where to begin. For one thing, why don't all workers make the minimum wage? Why, for example, don't greedy hospitals collude to keep the salaries of brain surgeons very low? Why don't the partners of law firms do the same to their junior colleagues?

The obvious answer is that competition would prevent this absurd outcome. If workers in an industry were truly being paid significantly less than what they added to the bottom line—this is what economists call their *marginal revenue product*—then outsiders would earn huge profits by jumping into the business and hiring away some of those workers with slightly higher pay. The process would continue until the workers were being paid what they were generally worth.

There is nothing peculiar to highly skilled workers in this story. The logic applies to burger flippers as much as it does to software engineers. Of course, most people who apply at McDonald's are far less productive than software engineers, and so they'll initially earn far less in a free market.

What happens if the government decides to set a minimum wage of $5 per hour and punish anyone who tries to hire a $3-per-hour worker? Will the company decide to kick in the difference and lose $2 per hour on the worker in question? Of course not. The company will lay off workers until the remaining ones are more productive. Now how exactly does this help unskilled teenagers?

Unions hurt the working man

Minimum wage laws and other "pro-labor" legislation can't make workers more productive, and actually end up hurting them. Union "closed shops" reduce incentives for employers to hire new workers and thus prevent very low-skilled workers from getting even entry-level jobs that can train them for higher things. Even for those workers who are helped by unions that reduce labor competition, it is only at the expense of other workers. In contrast, a rising tide of capitalist investment in a free market economy creates more employment and better working conditions for everyone.

In a purely free market, there would still be a role for labor unions, just as in a free market there is still a role for agents or managers who help their clients find work and negotiate their contracts. They are not always necessary (how often do you need an agent or a manager?) but they certainly have an important role in particular businesses.

A national labor union in a free market could assist, for example, a carpenter moving from New York to California, if its role were to help him find jobs befitting his expertise. For conveniences such as this, carpenters (particularly those with high skills) would gladly pay dues to belong to such a union, while many building contractors, homeowners, and other employers would pay higher wages for this particular union's carpenters if they had had good experiences with them in the past.

A Book You're Not Supposed to Read

Out of Work: Unemployment and Government in Twentieth-Century America by Richard Vedder and Lowell Gallaway; New York: New York University Press, 1997.

Unfortunately, this type of mutually beneficial relationship is not a good description of the American union experience. With a nod and a wink from the federal government, American unions achieve "results" for their members the same way a mafia don looks out for his family—by threatening violence.

How does a typical unionization proceed? The union comes into a company—a factory, let us say—with potential members, and launches a campaign of misinformation, telling the employees how exploited and underpaid they are. All these benighted workers need to do, they are told, is vote for the union to painlessly receive pay raises, medical benefits, more vacation, and so on. These goodies will in no way force layoffs or put the company at a competitive disadvantage; they will simply come out of the surplus the shareholders are skimming off the top. Now, during this process, management cannot tell the workers that raising wages 5 percent will require cutting back on overtime hours—to do so is an implicit threat and is illegal under U.S. labor law.

To continue our story, suppose that 85 percent of the workers want to join the union. What happens then? Surely the 85 percent join the union, the other 15 percent remain independent, and the company can then decide whether it wants to deal with the former group as a single entity, or whether it wants to lay off all those newly unionized workers and hire independent replacements, right? After all, employers must enjoy the same rights of association as employees, and the union doesn't own the factory or the shareholders' money...right?

What a Capitalist Said

"[C]apitalism is the only system that functions in a way which rewards rationality and penalizes all forms of irrationality....It is capitalism that gave mankind its first steps toward freedom and a rational way of life. It is capitalism that broke through national and racial barriers, by means of free trade. It is capitalism that abolished serfdom and slavery in all the civilized countries of the world."

Ayn Rand, *The Virtue of Selfishness*

Actually, this isn't the way it works. Under current law, our hypothetical firm would become unionized, and the 15 percent who were opposed would either have to join the union against their will or find another job. Down the road, if the union didn't find management compliant enough with its demands, it could organize a strike. And if the firm tried to hire replacements during the strike, the union members might literally beat these "scabs" as the poor saps just tried to enter the factory and go to work.

Give me a break!

To hear union advocates explain it, you'd think that in a purely free market, employees would have no lunch, no breaks, no vacation, no sick days, and (while we're at it) no bathrooms on the job site at all. Obviously this isn't true. Just as employers have to offer competitive wages to attract skilled workers, so too do they have to offer other benefits to retain a productive work force. If a certain frill—such as a bathroom—is "obvious," in the sense that workers would gladly take a small pay cut in order to

A Book You're Not Supposed to Read

Freedom in the Workplace: The Untold Story of Merit Shop Construction's Crusade against Compulsory Trade Unionism by Samuel Cook; Washington, DC: Regnery, 2005.

finance the additional perk, then the employer doesn't need a union or the government to tell him to make the profit-maximizing decision. And if a certain benefit *isn't* profitable—meaning that workers would rather forgo the perk than take the pay cut necessary to finance it—then forcing the employer to provide it only hurts the workers!

In short, unions can indeed acquire benefits for their members. But this isn't done—as it would be in a truly free market—through voluntary, cost-cutting measures or through improved productivity. Rather, unions achieve their goals through force, wielded directly by union goons or by the creation of de facto monopolies and vetoes on employers' rights to hire certain workers (under compulsory unionization), or by the might of the federal government acting on the unions' behalf. Because these threats and work stoppages don't make the workers more productive, unions achieve their gains only at the expense of the rest of society.

Chapter Four

THE CASE AGAINST ANTI-DISCRIMINATION LAWS

elf-appointed spokesmen for "oppressed" groups love to blame the free market for all the "inequities" of modern society. Were it not for benevolent government intervention, these people claim, blacks would still use separate water fountains and women could serve only as nurses and teachers. Yet as with other anti-capitalist myths, we will see that the true situation is precisely the opposite: the market contains powerful incentives for employers to make objective decisions based on merit, while government agencies face no such constraints.

The free market's "racist fee"

We need to be clear what we mean by discrimination when we say it is bad. In the most literal sense, *discrimination* is inevitable and good. An employer ought to be "discriminating" in that he should aim to hire people who are hardworking, talented, knowledgeable, trustworthy, and so on.

But even discrimination based on sex, race, or other "superficial" characteristics is often fine by any normal standards. Consider the award-winning film *The Hours*, in which one of the characters is the author Virginia Woolf. Now suppose Dustin Hoffman came in to audition for that part (a job that ultimately went to Nicole Kidman). Even if Hoffman

Guess what?

- The free market penalizes discrimination.

- The male/female "wage gap" is largely a myth.

- Real discrimination occurs at the hands of government and unions.

touted his portrayal of a woman in *Tootsie* as his credentials for the role of Virginia Woolf, a casting director would no doubt rule Hoffman out simply because, whatever his acting talent, his sex was a more important factor.

No one complains about this sort of discrimination.

Consider a different case: in the United States, black people constitute about 12.5 percent of the overall population, yet about 77 percent of NBA players are black. Is this prima facie evidence of gross racial bias in the hiring process for professional basketball? Again, obviously not.

What then do we mean when discussing discrimination in the labor market?

You might think we mean "prejudice"—or, more accurately, bigotry—but that's not necessarily true either. For example, it's possible that the late Marge Schott, controversial owner of the Cincinnati Reds, was, despite her protestations to the contrary, a genuine racist and supporter of Adolf Hitler, as some of her comments seemed to indicate. However, notwithstanding her pejorative description of employees Eric Davis and Dave Parker, Schott presumably didn't let her racial attitudes affect her hiring and salary decisions—after all, black players were among the stars on the team, and the Reds won the World Series five years after Schott was named president and CEO. Her hiring and salary policies seemed more concerned with success on the field and on the ledger sheet.

We care about workplace discrimination if an employer hires, rejects, promotes, or fires someone not because of his or her performance or potential, but because of his or her race, sex, or other irrelevant characteristic.

That's exactly where the free market provides the best solution. If employers make hiring and salary decisions based on criteria that are irrelevant to the success of the company, guess what? The free market punishes them. An employer who refused to hire, sell to, or deal with blacks, Hispanics, Jews, women, Catholics, or any other group would be harming himself, limiting his market, and shrinking his own pool of available talent and hence of productive managers and workers.

Discrimination is bad for business

Let's get specific. If an employer has an opening that pays $50,000 in salary, and the Christian applicant will bring in $51,000 in extra revenue to the firm while the Muslim applicant will bring in $55,000, then to discriminate against the creed of the latter will cost the employer $4,000 in potential profits. (The employer will make $1,000 by hiring the Christian but $5,000 by hiring the Muslim.) No government inspector or watchdog agency is required: by definition, discrimination is automatically "fined" in the free market.

In addition, not only does the market catch discrimination whenever it occurs, but the amount of the "fine" is also exactly proportional to the severity of the discrimination. If a businessman hires his nephew to paint his store, even though a stranger's kid would do the same job for $50 less, then the nepotism has cost him $50. But if the businessman hires his nephew to design the company's website and create a marketing campaign—rather than outsourcing these jobs to true professionals—the decision to "keep it in the family" will be far more expensive.

In short, employers are free to discriminate in the free market, but this discrimination certainly isn't free.

The "discriminating" customer

Employers pay a price when they hire people on the basis of some other criterion than productivity. But couldn't businessmen make profits by catering to prejudices held by *customers*? For example, if a restaurateur knows that many of his customers would object to being served by a black waitress, and that they would act on this prejudice by taking their

A Book You're Not Supposed to Read

The State against Blacks by Walter Williams; New York: McGraw-Hill, 1984.

business elsewhere, then it would be more profitable (assuming he had no fear of lawsuits or government fines) for him to hire a less-qualified white woman for the job.

But in cases like this the free market (even absent government fines) still punishes discrimination—only this time the *customer* pays the "racist fee": the customer pays extra (in the form of inferior service) to be served by a white waitress who is worse at her job than a better-qualified black candidate.

There is really nothing mysterious or inherently objectionable about this process per se. People pay for what they want all the time. People pay more to see a Broadway show than they do to see a community theater knockoff production, and they pay more to be served prime rib by extremely polite, well-dressed staff than to be tossed a burger by a rude teenager in a grease-soaked apron. In these contexts, to have "discriminating taste" is laudable.

A promoter will offer George Carlin far more money than, say, the watermelon-smashing Leo Gallagher, and the obvious explanation is that the public will pay more to see the comedy of the former. There is nothing "objective" about this preference, and indeed many Gallagher fans might consider it unfair. By the same token, it is undeniable that part of the financial success of Angelina Jolie, Jennifer Lopez, and Nicole Kidman is due to their beauty—these women make far more money than they would if they were horribly disfigured. Does this constitute discrimination against ugly singers or actresses?

Most people would probably answer by saying, "Yes, in a sense, but that's not what we mean when we say we're against discrimination." What people really mean by "discrimination" in the pejorative sense is acting on a preference that the critic doesn't possess himself. In short, most people don't want to watch movies with ugly stars, and so they don't much object to the obvious "bias" in Hollywood in favor of pretty people. But on the other hand, most people don't think it matters (or at least want to be people who think it doesn't matter) to be served by a Christian versus a Muslim, and so have no problem voting for politicians pledging to ban this type of preference.

Private property and the freedom of association

Government edicts attempting to curb "discrimination" underscore a contradiction in the American political landscape. On the one hand, people are supposedly free to form whatever associations they wish, free from government intimidation. Thus, if a racist has only white friends, and invites only white people to his dinner parties, the vast majority of Americans would conclude that while he is a reprehensible person, he shouldn't actually be fined (let alone imprisoned) for his actions, and shouldn't under court order have to invite blacks to his parties. "After all," some might say, "the guy owns his house and he can choose his own friends and have whoever he wants to parties so long as they don't disturb the peace. Sure, he's a jerk, but it's not a crime to be a jerk."

Yet when it comes to the racist's business, things are entirely different. Here, the vast majority of Americans don't think the man has the right to hire only white employees. Most Americans think that the government can fine him, and that a court can order him to hire black workers. Even though he may think he owns the real estate and other property associated with his business, our hypothetical racist is sadly mistaken; in effect the entire community owns

A Book You're Not Supposed to Read

Capitalism: The Cure for Racism by George Reisman; The Jefferson School of Philosophy, Economics & Psychology, 1992.

his property, and he is expected to act in accordance with their sense of racial justice.

There's nothing "affirmative" about affirmative action

One of the proposed remedies for racial and sexual discrimination is "affirmative action," whereby employers must strive to ensure that qualified minorities and women are considered for hiring or promotions. Proponents of affirmative action are quick to distinguish it from quotas—the law doesn't require that a firm choose a less-qualified black applicant for a job, only that the firm make every effort to make sure there isn't an equally qualified black applicant before hiring the white guy. Despite the official wording of the statutes, however, experience has shown that the easiest way for a company to demonstrate its commitment to affirmative

The Myth of the Male/Female "Wage Gap"

There is no male/female "salary gap" in the free market. Such gaps in wages that exist between men and women result from other relevant data, like job experience, educational background, different pay scales in different fields, and so on. The more one corrects for these crucial factors, the more the gap disappears. Indeed, according to Thomas Sowell, merely adjusting for marital status can eliminate the gap altogether in certain fields. Sowell finds that "never married" academic women are paid more than "never married" academic men. While it might be true that traditional marriage roles (with the husband as the provider and the wife as the mother and homemaker) favor a husband's career over a mother's, that isn't the fault of capitalism; and it's only a "fault" at all if you think a job in the marketplace is more important than the job of raising a family and caring for a home.[1]

action (and hence defend itself from lawsuits) is to hire in proportion to the racial mix of the surrounding community. Thus the zealous effort to alleviate past injustices has led to the institutionalization of genuine racial and sexual discrimination.

Ironically, affirmative action hurts the very groups it is supposed to help. For one thing, every time a black or other protected minority is hired or promoted, the surly white males who were passed over can blame it on affirmative action, even if the decision was based purely on merit. Perhaps more serious, by "breaking down barriers," affirmative action sets up the historically "disadvantaged" groups for failure. As Thomas Sowell explains:

> **Affirmative Action... on the Farm**
>
> "All animals are equal, but some animals are more equal than others."
>
> **George Orwell,** *Animal Farm*

> It makes a very real difference that 90 percent of the white MIT students score higher in math than the average black MIT student. A substantially higher percentage of the black students fail to finish MIT, and those who do graduate have substantially lower grade-point averages.
>
> The tragedy is that this waste—one-fourth of the black students don't graduate at MIT—is completely unnecessary. The average black student at MIT is well above the national average on math tests. He is just not in the stratospheric level of other MIT students.
>
> At most colleges, universities, or technical institutes, these same black students would be on the dean's list.
>
> In short, black students with every prospect of success are artificially turned into failures by being mismatched with their college. This is not peculiar to MIT. It is a nationwide phenomenon

among elite schools, who are more interested in having a good-looking body count from every group than they are in the price that has to be paid.

Everyone pays a very high price for this academic fad. Disadvantaged minority students pay the highest price of all. Asians may be lucky that they are not considered "minority."[2]

The problem, suffice it to say, is not with color-blind test scores that assess a student's chances for success in a subject, but with color-conscious admissions criteria that mismatch students and schools.

So everything's hunky-dory?

Naturally, a reader who is quite convinced of the prevalence of unjust racial and sexual discrimination would find this chapter's analysis absurd, for it seems to (attempt to) logically refute something that is quite evident to anyone with eyes. But the problem isn't with the arguments above. Unfortunately, neither the United States nor any other country has an entirely free labor market, and so we can't count on market forces to eradicate the unjust discrimination that offends most people.

It remains a mystery why leftists trust government to reform an unjust society. After all, any prejudices harbored by the people at large will be reflected in the government officials they elect. The only difference is that bureaucrats don't face the same free market penalties that employers (or customers) do for following their prejudices. (By the same token, kickbacks and other forms of corruption are far more dangerous in government than in the private sector, because shareholders have far more incentives than do congressmen to detect waste, fraud, and abuse.)

Indeed, the most horrible and "unfair" employment decisions in history—such as the persecution of academics during China's Cultural Revolution or the Nuremberg Laws of Nazi Germany—have occurred at the hands of governments. Chairman Mao and Adolf Hitler made such decisions because the perverse incentives of state control shielded them from the monumental damage they wreaked. In contrast, no matter how prejudiced he might be, Bill Gates would never decide to fire all his top software developers if they had different political views, or if they were of Semitic origin; such a decision would simply cost

A Book You're Not Supposed to Read

Reflections of an Affirmative Action Baby by Stephen L. Carter; New York: Basic Books, 1991.

too much. And if he did indulge such prejudices, he'd have to pay a steep economic price as talented Jewish and conservative software developers flooded to his competitors. Clearly discriminatory systems, such as apartheid in South Africa or Jim Crow laws in the Reconstruction-era American South, were set up by governments.

Another consideration is the role of labor unions. When the government gives a nod and a wink to union violence, we no longer have a free labor market, and thus we can't trust in market forces to penalize discrimination. For example, in a purely free market a building contractor would have no financial reason to prefer white construction workers to black. Even if the white crew in question (for whatever reason) were more talented, the black construction crew could offer to work for lower salaries, making them more attractive to employers, at least for less-skilled positions. Blacks would be on an equal footing with whites for job opportunities because they could compete on price. But if unions (made up, say, of predominantly white workers) were allowed to form picket lines and beat any "scabs" to a bloody pulp, then the building contractor has no choice but to hire unionized (and in this case, predominantly white) workers. Non-union blacks could be driven out of the market.

These are not abstract speculations. The Davis-Bacon Act of 1931 requires that all federally funded construction contracts pay "locally prevailing wages." The act was ostensibly pro-labor, but many cynics viewed it as a way to keep tax dollars from being funneled into the hands of black construction workers. In effect, the act made it illegal for black workers to submit a low bid for federal construction contracts, and thus awarding the contracts to the (more experienced but more expensive) white unions wouldn't appear discriminatory.

Women are also disproportionately hurt by "pro-labor" legislation. One of Bill Clinton's major coups, the Family and Medical Leave Act (FMLA) of 1993, guarantees employees up to twelve weeks of unpaid time off per year to care for a newborn, sick spouse, ailing parent, etc. The

Supporters of the Davis-Bacon Act of 1931

Congressman John Cochran of Missouri said he had "received numerous complaints in recent months about Southern contractors employing low-paid colored mechanics getting work and bringing the employees from the South."

Alabama congressman Clayton Allgood complained: "Reference has been made to a contractor from Alabama who went to New York with bootleg labor. This is a fact. That contractor has cheap colored labor that he transports, and he puts them in cabins, and it is labor of that sort that is in competition with white labor throughout the country."

Georgia congressman William Upshaw complained of the "superabundance or large aggregation of negro labor," which is a real problem "you are confronted with in any community."

New York congressman Robert Bacon replied, "I just mentioned the fact because that was the fact in this particular case, but the same would be true if you should bring in a lot of Mexican laborers or if you brought in any non-union laborers from any other state."

Other congressmen railed against "transient labor," or "cheap labor," or "cheap imported labor." American Federation of Labor president William Green translated what these words meant when he said, "(C)olored labor is being sought to demoralize wage rates."[3]

employer has to hold the worker's job, or provide a comparable one upon the employee's return. In addition, although the leave is unpaid, the employee is still entitled to benefits (such as health insurance) from the employer.

A Book You're Not Supposed to Read

Race and Culture: A World View by Thomas Sowell; New York: Basic Books, 1994.

Now what impact does the FMLA have on the labor market? The most obvious and immediate effect will be a reduction in salaries. Regardless of whether it is "the right thing to do," surely no one can deny that it is costly for the employer to grant such flexibility to employees. Now, since a firm won't hire a worker if it expects to lose money on the arrangement, that extra cost (due to the FMLA) must be offset by a lower salary.

Beyond this general effect, however, is a subtler one. Although the language of the statute does not differentiate between men and women—under the FMLA, new fathers are just as eligible as mothers to take twelve weeks off to care for the baby—employers know that a young, married female applicant for a job opening is statistically more likely to exercise her legal rights a few years down the road, as compared to a middle-aged bachelor or a married man (as married men are less likely to take time off to care for children than married women are). Thus the FMLA lowers the relative salaries of women compared to men, and especially lowers the salaries of young married women, since the law turns them into ticking financial liabilities.

There's a name for this—it's the law of unintended consequences, unless we think that the secret agenda of the FMLA was to discourage women from getting married and having children.

Chapter Five

✴ ✴ ✴ ✴ ✴ ✴ ✴ ✴

SLAVERY: PRODUCT OF CAPITALISM OR OF GOVERNMENT?

To some readers, the thesis of the last chapter—that free market capitalism is the antidote to racial and sexual discrimination—will seem ludicrous. After all, they might wonder, wasn't slavery the product of capitalism? This attitude is epitomized in the following quotation from Jenny Wahl's *Economic History* encyclopedia entry on slavery:

> Slavery is fundamentally an economic phenomenon. Throughout history, slavery has existed where it has been economically worthwhile to those in power. The principal example in modern times is the U.S. South. Nearly 4 million slaves with a market value of close to $4 billion lived in the U.S. just before the Civil War. Masters enjoyed rates of return on slaves comparable to those on other assets; cotton consumers, insurance companies, and industrial enterprises benefited from slavery as well.

There are many such claims that slavery was economically efficient; another work with this thesis is Robert William Fogel and Stanley L. Engerman's *Time On the Cross: The Economics of American Negro Slavery.*

Guess what?

- Slavery was propped up by government intervention.

- A free market would have eliminated slavery.

- Slavery made most whites poorer.

Government protects slavery

Despite this typical attitude, closer inspection shows that once again capitalism has gotten a bad rap, for it took government intervention to prop up the "peculiar institution." Most obviously, measures such as the fugitive slave laws (which dated back to at least 1793) took tax dollars paid by all in order to return the "property" of the privileged few plantation owners; here, as in so many other areas, politically powerful producers managed to foist the costs of their business operations (running slave plantations) onto the hapless public.

Drafting men into slave patrols was another device by which the Southern state governments shifted the costs of slavery onto the general public (and hence eased the burden on the slaveowners). As described by economist Mark Thornton, "The patrol statutes required all white males to participate in slave patrol duty.... Failure to participate in the patrols or carry out organizing responsibilities would result in a series of escalating fines."[1]

More subtle laws curtailing manumission (the practice of granting freedom to one's slaves, often bequeathed in a will) and forbidding the education of slaves also interfered with the normal operation of market forces. Wahl's encyclopedia article itself cites many other interferences with market forces (without calling them that), including laws that required slaveowners to guarantee that freed slaves would not become indigent public burdens, or that compelled slaveowners to free their slaves out of state, or that required the slaves themselves to pay fees, or that prevented slaves from hiring themselves out to others (though this last law was often ignored).

A Book You're Not Supposed to Read

The Real Lincoln: A New Look at Abraham Lincoln, His Agenda, and an Unnecessary War by Thomas DiLorenzo; Roseville, CA: Prima, 2002.

Slavery was declining before state interference

Ironically, government interference interrupted the market forces that would otherwise have gradually (and peacefully) spelled the demise of slavery. According to Thornton, "Between the 1790 and 1800 census, the free black population of America increased by over 82 percent and in the South Atlantic states by over 97 percent.... The total free population increased from 8.5 percent to almost 16 percent of the total black population between 1790 and 1810." However, as states instituted slave patrols and enacted restrictions on manumission (it actually made economic sense for masters to allow their slaves to buy their freedom, so pro-slave legislatures acted to discourage it) and the free movement of blacks, "the growth of the free black population decreased, fell below the rate of growth of the slave population, and was reduced to a trickle in the decade prior to the Civil War."

Slavery: Immoral, yes, but also inefficient!

The fundamental difference between free and slave labor is that freemen have an incentive to produce as much as possible. The slave, in contrast, will most likely perform the bare minimum necessary to avoid punishment. For this reason slave labor, as an institution, is inferior to an economy based on free labor—even from the point of view of the non-slaves. In the words of Ludwig von Mises:

> The price paid for the purchase of a slave is determined by the net yield expected from his employment... just as the price paid for a cow is determined by the net yield expected from its utilization. The owner of a slave does not pocket a specific revenue. For him there is no "exploitation" boon derived from the fact that the slave's work is not remunerated.... If one treats

men like cattle, one cannot squeeze out of them more than cattle-like performances. But it then becomes significant that man is physically weaker than oxen and horses, and that feeding and guarding a slave is, in proportion to the performance to be reaped, more expensive than feeding and guarding cattle. . . . If one asks from an unfree laborer human performances, one must provide him with specifically human inducements.[2]

And, as Mises points out, competitive free labor will always produce better products than slave labor, a free market economy will always perform better than a slave economy, and a slave economy simply cannot compete in a market that values quality goods.

But didn't it take the benevolence of the federal government to free the slaves? Yes, but only because other government ordinances had artificially maintained slavery in the antebellum South. (Another minor point: notice that it didn't take a bloody civil war anywhere outside the United

If You Have to Be a Slave . . . Better to Be Owned in the Private Sector!

"While it occasionally happened that a private slave owner [in the antebellum U.S. South] killed his slave . . . socialist slavery in Eastern Europe resulted in the murder of millions of civilians. Under private slave ownership the health and life expectancy of slaves generally increased. In the Soviet Empire healthcare standards steadily deteriorated and life expectancies actually declined in recent decades. The level of practical training and education of private slaves generally rose. That of socialist slaves fell. The rate of reproduction among privately owned slaves was positive. Among the slave populations of Eastern Europe it was generally negative."[3]

Hans-Hermann Hoppe, *Democracy: The God That Failed*

States to free slaves; the institution faded away peacefully as capitalism swept the world.)

If slavery was so profitable to the exploiters, then why was the free North able to crush the slave-ridden South? Why did Union fleets blockade the South and Northern factories churn out far greater supplies for troops, rather than vice versa? It is true that there were wealthy individual Southerners, and wealthy Southern cities, but the North's free labor economy and its focus on productive investment made it an industrial titan to the South's (comparative) rural backwater, in the same way that Europe and the United States are economic titans compared to the largely agricultural economies of the world.

This correlation between slavery and (relative) poverty isn't limited to the antebellum South, but is rather exhibited throughout world history:

> Both conservative apologists and radical critics of Western civilization have attempted to make the case that the institution of slavery made an important contribution to the economic and cultural development of the West.
>
> No nation in the Western Hemisphere . . . so prodigally consumed so many millions of slaves as Brazil. Yet, when Brazil became the last nation in the hemisphere to abolish the institution of slavery in 1888, it was still an economically underdeveloped country. Its later industrial and commercial development was largely the work of European immigrants, who accomplished a more general and enduring transformation of the Brazilian economy within two generations than had occurred during centuries of slavery. . . . In Europe, it was the nations in the western region of the continent, where slavery was abolished first, that led the continent and the world into the modern industrial age.[4]

The rising price of slaves

Those who deny that a free market would have eliminated slavery have an apparent trump card: the total market value of all slaves in the United States reached its peak (exceeding the value of the nation's railroads, according to some authors) immediately prior to the Civil War. Consequently, isn't it obvious that the institution was doing just fine, and that it would have continued indefinitely had not Union troops intervened?

Actually, no. For one thing, we should recognize that the rising market value of slaves is entirely consistent with the thesis that slavery was an inefficient system that wouldn't have lasted long in a truly free market. When an economist says that slave labor is inefficient, he always means relative to free labor. The claim isn't that output in the South would have been higher if all the slaves suddenly disappeared or dropped dead, but rather that output would have been higher if all the slaves were freed and allowed to voluntarily sell their labor to the employers of their choice.

Over time, with the discovery of new techniques and the accumulation of more machinery and other capital goods, the productivity of human labor—both free and slave—rose. Improvements in medicine, nutrition, and so on also increased life expectancy rates. Since a slave represented a lifetime reservoir of labor services, it is thus not surprising that his market value would go up over time. Indeed, from 1820 to 1856 the market price of a "prime" male slave in New Orleans rose from about $850 to over $1,200. But during the same time frame, nominal daily wage rates for unskilled labor in South Central states rose from about 73 cents to roughly 95 cents.[5] So of the 41

A Book You're Not Supposed to Read

Emancipating Slaves, Enslaving Free Men by Jeffrey Rogers Hummel; Peru, IL: Open Court, 1996.

percent rise in slave prices, at least 30 percent could be due to the growing productivity of labor in general.

The rising price of slaves by itself means nothing. The issue under dispute is whether slave labor was more efficient than free labor, and so to test this we would need to compare (at the very least) the growth in slave prices with the growth in wage rates, and to make an adjustment for increased life expectancy rates as well as possible changes in interest rates. Ideally, we would want to compare the profitability of two firms that were identical in all respects except that one employed slave labor while the other hired freemen. And even then statistical analyses gauging the "success" of slavery would have to factor in the costs of the government regulations that propped up slavery.

If slavery is so inefficient, then why did it exist at all?

This question is akin to asking, "If we all agree that war is hell, why do humans keep starting wars?" The sad fact is, people are motivated by all sorts of bad ideas that keep us poorer than we otherwise could be. Beyond this general fact of the human condition, here's another: people will always lobby the government for privileges, even though everyone would be better off if *all* privileges were eliminated. The institution of slavery was just a particularly horrific consequence of this fact.

Chapter Six

HOW CAPITALISM WILL SAVE THE ENVIRONMENT

Among all its other sins, the capitalistic system allegedly squanders natural resources and destroys Mother Earth. The environmental activists tell us that the market's unfettered greed led to the near extinction of the buffalo and that the industrialists' focus on the bottom line gives us global warming and acid rain. Were it not for the wise (but inadequate) government interventions in the past, we would have long since run out of aluminum for our soda cans—but this would be irrelevant as we'd be dead from a nuclear plant meltdown.

In fact, the environmentalist warnings are nonsense. As reputable scientists will testify, the earth is not on the brink of destruction. Moreover, the free market encourages sound conservation and stewardship, while government policies cause waste and needless pollution.

Rhinos versus cows

Private property rights encourage people to conserve resources for future use much more than any government regulations do. Pop quiz: What's the difference between bald eagles, white rhinos, and giant pandas on one hand, versus talking parrots, dairy cows, and thoroughbred horses on the

Guess what?

- Free markets encourage conservation.

- The best way to save endangered species is to make them commodities.

- Known reserves of oil rose during the twentieth century.

- Communist countries are the most polluted.

other? Answer #1: All of the former are endangered species, while the latter are in plentiful supply. Answer #2: It is illegal to trade in the former, while the latter are bought and sold in the open market.

This is no coincidence. When someone has well-defined and secure property rights in a reproducible resource, he has every incentive to ensure its continued existence. The government doesn't need to assess fines on ranchers who foolishly slaughter every last cow the moment beef prices rise; this would be as unheard of as a farmer who ate all the seed corn.

In contrast, when the government—or "the public"—owns a resource, it's as if no one owns it. The political rulers of African nations have little incentive to crack down on poachers, since (generally speaking) they don't personally benefit from maintaining the stocks of rhinos and other endangered species. In contrast, we never see press releases from the World Conservation Union concerning theft of cattle—the animals' owners would see to it that any would-be cow poachers were dealt justice, *Lonesome Dove*–style.

Conservation for whom?

There is a strange paradox in the typical conservationist worldview. The present generation is berated for its selfish consumption of scarce resources such as oil and natural gas; every trip to the pump today translates into fewer car trips for the grandkids fifty years from now.

But wait just a second. Suppose we heed the lectures and cut our oil consumption by a million barrels per year. Does that mean our grandchildren get to consume that much more? If they did, wouldn't they be stealing oil from *their* grandchildren—as environmentalists in fifty years would no doubt remind them?

When it comes to nonrenewable resources, every unit consumed is, in principle, infinitely costly in the sense that a limitless number of future humans could have benefited from it, but now won't have the opportunity. Yet thinking in these terms leads to the absurd outcome that no one ever gets to benefit from the resource; all the oil would sit in the ground uselessly forever because everyone would feel too guilty to burn a single drop.

Private property rights and market prices provide the answer to this conundrum. The owner of an oil field, copper mine, or other finite resource extracts and sells the commodity at the rate that maximizes the

Capitalism Cleans Up

"The world in which I spent my early years was a very smelly place. The prevailing odors were of horse manure, human sweat, and unwashed bodies. A daily shower was unknown; at most there was the Saturday night bath.

Indoors the air was generally musty and permeated by the sweetly acrid stench of kerosene lamps and coal fires. It was the era of the horse and buggy, the outhouse, and dirt. Depending upon the weather, it was either dusty or muddy. Only a few urban streets were paved—with cobblestones or brick. Mud puddles and corrugated ruts or 'corduroy roads' were the potholes of my youth.

Automobiles had been invented, of course, but they were few in number, handcrafted, and expensive enough so that only the rich could afford them. I was nearly ten years old when the Model T began to put America on wheels. Indeed, Mr. Henry Ford made a greater contribution to public health than most practitioners of science by introducing an affordable auto—which led to the eventual elimination of horse manure from public streets."

Dixy Lee Ray, *Trashing the Planet*

present market value of the resource. As the supply dwindles, this pushes up the price, which encourages more economical usage and the search for alternatives. Future generations lay their claim to (some of) today's oil by the money they'll spend on gasoline. The oil companies won't forget to reserve some oil for the people in 2025, just as they never forget to ship oil to the people in Boise, Idaho.

We'll cross that bridge when we get to it

The hysterical warnings about resource depletion overlook the fact that businesses will find new supplies and develop alternative technologies,

The Waste of "Public" Resources: An All Too Common Tragedy

Economists describe the fate of communally owned resources as a "tragedy of the commons," after a famous article by Garrett Hardin. In Hardin's original historical example, before the great enclosures of pasture lands, herders would systematically allow their animals to overgraze, i.e. to eat more grass than would allow the pasture to sustain itself. In modern times, communal lakes and streams are plagued by overfishing and not enough fish are left in the water to sustain the population. Everyone is aware of the problem, but no one has the incentive to change; even if an individual fisherman limits his catch, that won't prevent the next one from taking the fish himself. The way to solve the tragedy of the commons is to convert the public resource into private property. With privately owned and managed bodies of water, over-fishing would be as obsolete as overgrazing.

but only when it's profitable for them to do so. It takes time and other scarce resources to locate a new oil field and assess its likely capacity. Consequently, at any given time humans have identified only a fraction of the available supplies of oil, natural gas, and other nonrenewable resources, because there's no need to look for more oil when the stockpile we've already found will last for decades.

The practical limit to resource extraction is an economic, not a technical constraint. Oil wells and copper mines are abandoned well before they are exhausted, because it doesn't pay to extract every last barrel of oil or ounce of copper. But as new technologies are developed, extraction costs can be reduced, effectively multiplying the economically relevant reserves.

A Book You're Not Supposed to Read

Energy: The Master Resource by Robert L. Bradley, Jr. and Richard W. Fulmer; Dubuque, IA: Kendall/Hunt Publishing Company, 2004.

Now if government interferes with property rights—that is, if government regulation (price controls) or threats (nationalization) make the owner of an oil field feel his rights over his oil are insecure—he will work to pump and sell the oil as fast as he can to make profits while he can. If, on the other hand, he feels that his property rights are very secure, he is in no rush to pump the oil and can decide what level of extraction best makes sense compared to the money he could make off other investments. So in other words, meddling with property rights causes faster oil extraction.

The ultimate bet: Ehrlich bombs

When it comes to professional scaremongering, accuracy in predictions is not a job requirement. No one illustrates this better than Paul Ehrlich, author of the 1968 classic *The Population Bomb*. Ehrlich wrote that "the battle to feed all of humanity is over.... In the 1970s and 1980s hundreds of millions of people will starve to death in spite of any crash programs embarked upon now."

Julian Simon held the completely opposite view, considering the human mind to be the "ultimate resource." A rising population meant more geniuses to solve the practical problems of food production and cramped living quarters. Simon's proof that additional people contribute more to society than they take? As population grows, so do real wage rates.

In contrast, resources other than human labor were becoming less important over time, as gauged by their falling prices (adjusting for inflation). Indeed, in 1980 Simon made a famous wager with Ehrlich: they would specify a quantity of five metals worth $1,000 in 1980, and then check on the (inflation-adjusted) price in 1990. If it went up, Ehrlich would win. If the real price of the metals went down, Simon would win. (The loser had to mail the winner a check equal to the price change.) As it turned out, the prices of copper, chrome, nickel, tin, and tungsten fell so much that even ignoring inflation, Simon won the bet. There is one more relevant fact: Simon let Ehrlich (assisted by several physicists) pick the five metals for the wager.

The Confidence of a Capitalist

Julian Simon was so confident in his belief that commodity prices—for any commodity—would fall over time that he initially offered to bet Paul Ehrlich $10,000 on the proposition. Ehrlich and his colleagues—including two Berkeley physicists—revised the bet to $1,000. In October 1990, Paul Ehrlich mailed Julian Simon a check for $576.07 to settle the wager in Simon's favor.

Recycle? Or dump?

Contrary to the Earth Day rhetoric, the issue of recycling is not a moral issue but an economic one. After a product has been used, whether it should be salvaged and recycled to make another product or tossed in the trash isn't simply a matter of chemistry or biology. Before we can sensibly answer the question, we need to know the relevant market prices. All things considered, if it's cheaper to dispose of the used item and make a new one from virgin materials, then it would be wasteful (in a very real sense) to recycle the product. On the other hand, if the circumstances change (maybe landfills reach their capacity, or the virgin material runs low), it may make sense to begin recycling even though it wasn't done in the past.

The crucial point is that "recycling" wasn't an invention of the tree-huggers. Anyone who has worked for a large business

Oil Reserves: Less Is More

Proven worldwide reserves of crude oil were estimated at 51 billion barrels at the end of 1944. By 2002, after fifty-eight years of "myopic" gas guzzling, the official figure for proven reserves had *grown* to 1,266 billion barrels worldwide.[1]

knows that recycling happens all the time, without any prodding from the government. For example, grocery stores go through a tremendous number of cardboard boxes. Rather than simply throwing them out, they instead crush the boxes and then sell them (by weight) to the appropriate companies. Factories too will salvage metals and other valuable scrap items because companies exist that buy such "trash," melt it down, and reuse it.

There is a limit to this process, however. Companies don't (and shouldn't) recycle everything. For example, the shipping labels on the boxes that a company receives could in principle be recycled, but it wouldn't be worth the hassle—even though recycling the box might be. When the 60-watt bulb in the secretary's lamp goes out, it might be fine to toss it, even though her company as a rule doesn't throw out the huge fluorescent bulbs used on the plant floor. To take an extreme example that illustrates the point nicely: a law office might have recycle bins for the reams of computer paper its staff uses, but it certainly would instruct its employees to throw out used tissues and toilet paper!

What happens when the government imposes an artificial reward for recycling? In this case it distorts the true signals offered by market prices

Oil Is Running Out—This Time, We Mean It

- In 1885 the U.S. Geological Survey said there was little or no chance of discovering oil in California.
- In 1914 an official of the U.S. Bureau of Mines estimated total future production at only 5.7 billion barrels. (By 1984 more than 34 billion barrels had been produced.)
- In 1920 the director of the U.S. Geological Survey predicted that the U.S. had nearly reached peak production. (By 1948 production was over four times the 1920 rate.)
- In 1939 the Interior Department predicted U.S. oil supplies would last thirteen years.
- In 1949 the secretary of the interior predicted that the end of U.S. oil supplies was almost in sight.[2]

and thus causes people to behave inefficiently. For example, absent government intervention, individual households wouldn't recycle soda or beer cans, because the market value of the salvageable aluminum is far too low to make it worth the effort to save the cans (possibly after rinsing them), load them in the car, and drive them to the recycling center. But by imposing a five- or ten-cent deposit, the government makes it worthwhile for many people to recycle. This number, however, is completely fictitious; it doesn't represent the true economic value of the aluminum that can be salvaged from a can. So instead of throwing the cans into a dump—the economical outcome—we have the ridiculous situation of millions of households devoting time to saving their cans, and thousands of employees at grocery stores having to deal with the returns. There are now even special machines with the sole purpose of collecting returned cans and bottles; some models of these "reverse vending machines" can cost over $35,000.

If the sheer waste and stupidity of this scenario isn't obvious, the reader should try a different example. Suppose that the government charged a quarter deposit on ballpoint pens; when the pen ran dry, the consumer could return it for a "full" refund. Or what about the circular tab on a plastic milk carton that ensures it hasn't been opened? Or while we're at it, what about the clear plastic security strips that come on new CD or DVD cases? The government could tack a $1 deposit on them, adding yet another priority to Americans' lives and giving the homeless another item for which to scour garbage cans.

A Book You're Not Supposed to Read

Environmental Overkill: Whatever Happened to Common Sense? by Dixy Lee Ray; Washington, DC: Regnery, 1993.

Finally, consider the lack of market pricing for garbage. If your neighbors asked you if they could ditch their banana peels, coffee filters, dirty diapers, and broken hubcaps in the empty lot you own on the edge of town, you probably would ask to be compensated—just as a storage facility would charge. The more the neighbor wanted to throw out, the more you would charge.

But when the county or town government takes your trash, they often don't charge you by the pound. However much you reuse, reduce, and use cloth diapers you pay the same taxes to your sanitation department as your neighbor who seems to be tossing out five bags of trash a day. If you were paying by the pound for trash, you might think twice before tossing out a broken pitcher that could make a fine planter.

The pollution of activist government

Some readers may be surprised to learn that it was late nineteenth and early twentieth century government intervention (aimed at

A Book You're Not Supposed to Read

Economics and the Environment: A Reconciliation, ed. Walter Block; Vancouver: Fraser Institute, 1990.

promoting "industrialization") that overturned common-law nuisance lawsuits against factory owners and other polluters. Contrary to popular belief, the advocate of the free market doesn't think corporations should be given a green light to pollute. The term "free enterprise" doesn't imply that a big company can use electricity or other resources without paying for them; in a society with secure property rights, an industrialist who dumped chemicals in a river would have to first make arrangements with the river's owners.

In any case, the hysterics over global warming, the ozone hole, and acid rain have been debunked countless times by reputable scientists. (Christopher Horner's *Politically Incorrect Guide™ to Global Warming and Environmentalism* is a good place to start.) But for our purposes it's important to note that capitalist economies make for cleaner environments than do socialist ones. If you wanted to find real environmental catastrophes, you'd look not at the United States or Western Europe but at the former members of the Soviet Union and its Eastern bloc. After all, in contrast to the phony scare over Three Mile Island, dozens of people really did die during the Chernobyl nuclear reactor accident (though even here, not necessarily from radiation). According to Ruben Mnatsakanian, professor of environmental sciences and policy at the Central European University in Budapest:

> The mountains of solid wastes, and lakes of liquid ones, near most heavy industry in Poland, the Czech Republic, the former German Democratic Republic, Ukraine, Russia, Kazakhstan, Estonia, and other countries are probably the most visible environmental legacy of the former [Soviet] system. Storing wastes

in open ponds, or on the ground (with practically no protection against percolation), was common.

Appalling facts on the production and storage of chemical weapons in Russia (kept absolutely secret during Soviet times) have recently become known. Seven factories produced chemical weapons in five cities—Berezniki, Chapaevsk, Dzherzhinsk, Volgograd and Novocheboksarsk. The last four are on the banks of the Volga—Europe's largest river and the source of drinking water for millions of people. Production, testing, and storage of chemical weapons were accompanied by numerous violations of safety rules. In 1990–1992—before it signed the International Convention on Chemical Weapons—Russia announced that it had 40,000 tonnes of poisonous substances, including 32,000 tonnes of phosphorous-organic compounds.

A Book You're Not Supposed to Read

Trashing the Planet: How Science Can Help Us Deal with Acid Rain, Depletion of the Ozone, and Nuclear Waste (Among Other Things) by Dixy Lee Ray; New York: Perennial, 1992.

As this chapter has demonstrated, the environmentalist attacks on capitalism are dead wrong. Market prices foster the proper balance between recycling and refuse, in contrast to arbitrary government campaigns. In practice, the capitalist economies have enjoyed steady improvement in environmental quality, while the totalitarian governments have been the worst desecrators of the planet.

Chapter Seven

ENSURING SAFETY:
THE MARKET OR BIG BROTHER?

Even among people who are generally sympathetic to the market economy, it is quite typical to reject *complete* laissez-faire—surely the government needs to establish and enforce some basic standards of quality and safety, right? Otherwise, laborers would be forced to work in death traps and the average consumer would be at the mercy of medical quacks. Consider the typical historical treatment of the notorious 1911 Triangle Fire disaster:

> The fire at the Triangle Waist Company in New York City, which claimed the lives of 146 young immigrant workers, is one of the worst disasters since the beginning of the Industrial Revolution. This incident has had great significance to this day because it highlights the inhumane working conditions to which industrial workers can be subjected. To many, its horrors epitomize the extremes of industrialism. The tragedy still dwells in the collective memory of the nation and of the international labor movement. The victims of the tragedy are still celebrated as martyrs at the hands of industrial greed.[1]

As with the other areas we've explored so far, here too the typical understanding is exactly backward. Even an "unregulated" market has

Guess what?

- Market forces protect workers and consumers.

- The American Medical Association is a cartel that raises medical costs.

- Zoning regulations raise crime rates in big cities.

- After a plane crash, the FAA gets *more* funding.

incentives to make product quality and safety a top priority for profit-hungry entrepreneurs. In contrast, government-imposed standards are not the magic panacea that most people assume. Indeed, political "remedies" are often worse than the disease.

There's always a trade-off...

Heartless as it may seem, we must acknowledge the fact that safety is costly. Let's consider the Triangle Fire case. Here the industrialists involved were vilified because they didn't spend enough on their employees' welfare. According to workers who escaped, the ninth-floor doors to the stairwell were locked, and the fire escape couldn't handle the number of people trying to use it. If only the owners had spent more money on precautions, dozens of lives could have been saved.

This just raises the question, however, of who was supposed to pay for these improvements. Contrary to union propaganda, in a competitive market workers generally get paid according to how much extra revenue they bring in to the company. If the employers are forced to shell out money when they hire workers (because more workers require additional precautions), this ultimately means smaller paychecks for the workers. Naturally, after the fact, the workers at the Triangle Shirtwaist Company would have gladly given up some of their pay in exchange for better conditions. But what of the thousands of other workers of the time, who didn't suffer the terrible catastrophe?

Here the paternalist liberal faces a conundrum: If the poor immigrant workers in 1911 really would have preferred lower paychecks in order to finance safer working conditions, then why did the government need to enforce the new codes? If the workers really would have accepted lower paychecks, then the precautions wouldn't have cost the owners anything out of pocket. On the other hand, what if the poor workers (as seems to be the case) preferred to take their chances, and suffered admittedly horrible conditions in exchange for slightly higher wages? Who are we to second-guess this decision?

From our comfortable vantage point, the decisions of relatively impoverished workers in the early 1900s seem shortsighted and reckless indeed. But by the same token, most people in the year 2100 will no doubt be shocked that we "savages" allowed humans (rather than robots) to work in coal mines.

Market safety

Just as a thought experiment, let's imagine the "anarchy" of a completely unregulated (by government) marketplace, where there are no labeling requirements, no building fire codes, no licensing requirements for brain surgeons, and so forth. Would it be as brutal as most people think?

Certainly not. Even if businesses were totally "unregulated," we're still assuming a basic framework of law and property rights, so firms would still have to persuade customers to buy their wares. In this environment, would it be a smart business move for McDonald's to use spoiled meat, or for Bayer to sell aspirin bottles full of placebos? Even if there were no legal sanctions against such fraudulent actions, it's clear that major corporations would make more profit by ensuring the quality of their products. For one thing, a company can't get repeat business if it sickens or kills its own customers!

Beyond this ultimate check of consumer boycott, a modern market economy has more sophisticated methods for protecting consumers. Most obvious are various rating services such as *Consumer Reports* magazine, or Underwriters Laboratories (whose seal of approval, UL, is displayed on light bulb packages and other electronics equipment). With the rise of the Internet, concerned buyers can conduct research (to see customer reviews, price quotes, and so forth) before making a purchase from an unfamiliar vendor.

Large intermediaries ("middlemen") often serve a vital role in protecting the consumer. For example, in addition to offering low prices, Wal-Mart also acts as a buffer between the relatively ignorant consumer and

Free Market Protection:
It's Everywhere You Want to Be

Ironically, credit card companies—no friends of Ralph Nader here!—also protect consumers from fraud. As attorney J. H. Huebert explains:

[Visa and MasterCard] know that the presence of their logos on merchants' doors and in advertisements is interpreted as a seal of approval, even if not intended as such. It is not good for Visa and the other brands to appear to be associated with crooks or anything else unpleasant to consumers. Thus the card companies have created their own system for pleasing consumers who have problems with credit transactions. This is called the chargeback.

Under the card companies' chargeback procedures, a consumer can inform his card issuer of his dispute and the issuer will then help him settle things. To begin chargeback proceedings, a cardholder files a complaint for free, using a form provided by the card company. (It is often included on the back of each month's billing statement.) On receiving the complaint, the card company may ask the cardholder for documentation to support his claim. If he appears to have a legitimate grievance, the bank will then initiate a chargeback against the merchant's bank—that is, the cardholder's bank will take the money back from the merchant's bank. The merchant's bank has no choice but to allow this because each bank in each card system has contractually agreed to these recourse procedures.[2]

the thousands of suppliers whose products fill its shelves. The average shopper is certainly in no position to evaluate produce from different growers in Florida, meat from different slaughterhouses in Chicago, and television sets from different manufacturers in China—but Wal-Mart has employees who are quite knowledgeable in each of these areas. Wal-Mart and other large retailers are in business for the long haul, and will succeed only if they can convince customers to trust them for all their shopping needs. It would be incredibly foolish for a large chain to try to make a few thousand dollars by carrying a cheap but defective lamp that might electrocute the user. Any short-term gains would be more than offset by the loss of goodwill in the community.

The regulators: Third-party guarantors

In this chapter I've twice put the word "unregulated" in quotation marks because in a market economy there are thousands, if not millions, of privately enforced rules and standards providing oversight and "regulation" to protect customers and the public. Underwriters Laboratories is just one example; there are countless others. For example, in the financial sector, ratings agencies such as Moody's provide expert evaluations of the creditworthiness of corporations and governments that issue bonds. Online clearinghouses such as eBay provide ratings for vendors and individuals to minimize fraud, while retailers such as Amazon employ encryption techniques to help protect their customers' sensitive information.

When it comes to private analogs of official government regulatory bodies, perhaps the best example is an insurance company. For example, imagine an airline industry that had no government oversight. Even so, the major carriers would no doubt have to offer, as part of their standard product, an indemnification clause in the event of a crash or other accident. For the sake of argument, perhaps the industry standard promises $1 million to the estate of anyone who dies in a plane crash.

Now this is a major potential liability, especially if the company has a fleet of jumbo jets making dozens of flights per day. Sheer conservatism (as well as the insistence of customers) would compel the airline to take out an insurance policy to protect its shareholders in the event of a crash.

Of course, the insurance company would insist on a hefty premium for taking on such a huge risk. But beyond this, it might also insist on other concessions. For example, the insurer might require that all the airline's pilots be certified by a reputable organization and that they undergo periodic drug testing. The insurer might also require that the airline buy jets only from recognized manufacturers. Indeed, to qualify for the lowest premiums, the airline might allow random inspections of its maintenance logs and other operations, and might even agree to pay specified fines on the basis of these surprise visits. Contrary to popular belief, a free market in air travel wouldn't rely on "vigilant" consumers keeping track of airline crash statistics. No, the system would be quite safe so long as most consumers insisted on indemnification in the event of a crash. The expert personnel at the insurance companies would take care of the rest.

Good Economics

"The bad economist sees only what immediately strikes the eye; the good economist also looks beyond. The bad economist sees only the direct consequences of a proposed course; the good economist looks also at the longer and indirect consequences. The bad economist sees only what the effect of a given policy has been or will be on one particular group; the good economist inquires also what the effect of the policy will be on all groups."

Henry Hazlitt, *Economics in One Lesson*

These considerations are not pure fancy. They are being practiced (to a greater or lesser extent) in the present, by real insurance companies. Anyone who has gotten cheaper homeowners' insurance because of smoke detectors or deadbolts, or who has given up smoking because of life insurance premiums, will recognize the pattern. The fundamental difference between private "regulators" versus government bureaucrats is that the former will last only if they are effective. If the insurance company's inspectors, for example, take kickbacks from the airlines and overlook cost-cutting but dangerous maintenance procedures, this corruption will be rooted out after the first plane crash. The insurer will lose hundreds of millions of dollars (certainly more than the total value of the kickbacks), and other airlines will advertise their superior standards and lure away passengers.

In contrast, let's analyze the present, government-regulated market for air travel. Consider the ValuJet disaster on May 11, 1996, when a crash in the Everglades killed all 110 people aboard Flight 592. The crash was particularly scandalous because of ValuJet's alleged systematic disregard for safety before the disaster. Now at the time of the crash, the Federal Aviation Administration (FAA) had been in place for thirty years (even more if we count its predecessors, such as the Federal Aviation Agency and the Civil Aeronautics Authority). Naturally, as its own website declares, one of the chief responsibilities of the FAA is the "continued airworthiness of aircraft." Indeed, if one had asked the average person on the day before the crash, "Why don't we abolish the FAA and have a free market in air travel?" the response would be a horrified, "Because then there would be plane crashes all the time!"

Given that the ostensible purpose of the FAA is to prevent (or reduce) plane crashes, one would think that this example of an unsafe company being given the green light by the government—immediately after the crash, Secretary of Transportation Frederico Peña reportedly said, "I would fly ValuJet tomorrow"—would count as a strike against it. To be

A Book You're Not Supposed to Read

Free to Choose: A Personal Statement by Milton and Rose Friedman; New York: Harcourt Brace Jovanovich, 1980.

sure, this alone wouldn't prove the case for unfettered free markets; one would first need to speculate on how many crashes would occur in that system and compare it to the number occurring under government regulation. But the point is, it should count against the government when a plane crashes under its supervision.

Yet this isn't what happens in the real world. Indeed, after the ValuJet crash there were outcries for the FAA to get *more* funding. The cozy relationship between ValuJet and its government regulators was labeled "the free market." As the socialists at the International Workers Bulletin tell us: "The death of the 110 men, women and children on board Flight 592 was the tragic outcome of a process that began in August 1981, when President Ronald Reagan fired 13,000 members of the Professional Air Traffic Controllers Organization who had gone on strike to fight for decent working conditions and increased staffing."[3]

This systematic hatred of capitalism isn't simply unfair or irrational—it actually undermines the very oversight that the concerned op-ed writers and socialist theorists desire! To reiterate: In a purely private setting, where all contractual relationships are voluntary and property rights are strictly enforced, any third-party agency that provided poor oversight would quickly go out of business. In contrast, when the government assumes the responsibility for safe air travel, its incompetence or corruption is rewarded with more money. It doesn't take a cynic to recognize that the former system will provide more safety than the latter.

Is there a doctor in the house?

The standard case for government purity and quality oversight, such as provided by the Food and Drug Administration (FDA), couldn't be simpler: The government imposes penalties on companies that try to sell dangerous products. How could this possibly hurt? If the market would have provided quality goods anyway, then the FDA is at worst irrelevant; while if it does make a difference, then it's obviously increasing safety. Right?

The situation is much more complicated than that. Actual medical products cannot be simply classified as "safe" or "dangerous." For example, suppose a new treatment promises an 80 percent chance of curing a certain type of cancer, but also poses a 1 percent chance of a stroke. Will the approval of this treatment increase or decrease "safety"? Is it "healthful" or not?

These are not merely philosophical questions. By making such decisions, the FDA removes the option of experimental drugs and techniques. In response to the thalidomide tragedies of the late 1950s, in 1962 the FDA beefed up its "standards" for drug approval. But such measures had a definite cost, as Milton Friedman pointed out in 1979:

> [T]he number of "new chemical entities" introduced each year has fallen by more than 50 percent since 1962. Equally important, it now takes much longer for a new drug to be approved and, partly as a result, the cost of developing a new drug has been multiplied manyfold. According to one estimate for the 1950s and early 1960s, it then cost about half a million dollars and took about twenty-five months to develop a new drug and bring it to market.... By 1978, "it [was] costing $54 million and about eight years of effort to bring a drug to market"—a hundredfold increase in cost and quadrupling of time, compared with a doubling of prices in general. As a result, drug companies can no longer afford to develop new drugs in the United States for patients with rare diseases. Increasingly, they must rely on drugs with high volume sales. The United States,

long a leader in the development of new drugs, is rapidly taking a back seat. And we cannot even benefit fully from developments abroad because the FDA typically does not accept evidence from abroad as proof of effectiveness.[4]

In addition to pointing out the drawbacks of the FDA, Friedman was also one of the earliest and harshest critics of occupational licensing, even in the apparently "obvious" case of medicine. For one thing, reducing the number of officially sanctioned doctors raises the price of medical care; many cynical observers of the American Medical Association (AMA) argue that its stringent qualifications have more to do with restricting competition rather than protecting patients. This is not merely an economic consideration; if there are fewer doctors (even though they may be the best of the best), patients will receive less total medical care. Friedman draws an analogy between medicine and automobiles: if the government insisted that no car below the standards of a Cadillac could be sold, this would not really raise the quality of car transportation in the U.S.

As Friedman points out, licensing doctors stifles research in unapproved areas, discourages them from testifying against each other in malpractice suits, and creates a sort of labor union problem where skilled doctors waste time performing routine medical procedures that, were it not for AMA rules, could be handled by nurses. But if we had a free market, Friedman argues, we could have "department stores of medicine" where specialized firms would act as intermediaries between patient and doctor. Friedman concludes:

> My aim is only to show by example that there are many alternatives to the present organization of practice. The impossibility of any individual or small group conceiving of all the possibilities, let alone evaluating their merits, is the great argument against central government planning and against arrange-

ments such as professional monopolies that limit the possibilities of experimentation. On the other side, the great argument
for the market is its tolerance of diversity; its ability to utilize
a wide range of special knowledge and capacity. It renders special groups impotent to prevent experimentation and permits
the customers and not the producers to decide what will serve
the customers best.[5]

Safety: Taking it to the streets

As the above quotation reminds us, one of the biggest objections to
bureaucratic "solutions" is that they often cause unintended consequences. By their very nature, these drawbacks to political intervention
cannot be predicted beforehand, at least in their specifics. But countless
examples have convinced many analysts that whenever the government
gets involved in a new area, overriding the voluntary and peaceful organization that had developed spontaneously, bad things will occur.

Here's a particularly interesting example: zoning legislation can
increase crime rates. The intent of the busybody regulators is understandable; they feel that in the "anarchy" of an unregulated real estate market,
businesses would be interspersed with residential property, especially in
large cities. Surely most people would dislike this outcome, and would
prefer responsible planning by the experts,
right?

Despite their possibly noble intentions,
the end result of city planning was exactly
the opposite: neighborhoods that were the
most carefully "engineered" were the ones
that ended up the most decrepit. The late
Jane Jacobs, in her 1961 classic *The Death
and Life of Great American Cities*, which is

A Book You're Not Supposed to Read

The Death and Life of Great American Cities
by Jane Jacobs; New York: Random House,
1961.

itself a manifesto that proclaims to be "an attack on current city planning and rebuilding," explained the surprising connection between zoning regulation and crime. She pointed out that public safety is best ensured when people voluntarily look after their own streets, and where stores, bars, and restaurants (open night and day) and public spaces are all jostled together, because it gives residents, business owners, and customers a mutual interest in ensuring safety, a complex interaction of unexpected "neighborhood watch" mutual support. Bureaucrat-planned zoning, however, breaks up this mutual support, this interaction between business owner, customer, and resident that is a natural form of neighborhood policing. In a touching eulogy, the Manhattan Institute's Howard Husock explained Jacobs's subtle understanding:

> To get Jane Jacobs right, start with her reasons for opposing urban renewal. Her opposition was not primarily based on aesthetic and planning concerns, though there is no doubt that the design of public housing deeply concerned and offended her. In her view, the quintessential housing-project design of the high-rise tower set in a plaza or park defied common sense. Plazas that people don't regularly traverse for a wide range of reasons—some going to work, some to the library, some to their homes—are apt to become dangerous gauntlets, as are the long corridors in high-rises, where the neighborly eyes Jacobs found watching the street in old neighborhoods are absent. The wealthy might be able to afford doormen and security patrols, but, Jacobs made clear, the less affluent need the self-policing that older, unplanned neighborhoods can provide.[6]

Anyone who has lived in a big city can recognize the truth in Jacobs's analysis. When "expert" planners divide a city into zones, with certain areas set aside for commercial development and others for residential, and construct giant housing projects and artificial "public" areas, they destroy precisely those mechanisms that naturally, though unintention-ally, serve to produce public safety. Is the hatred of commerce so strong that the liberals are willing to tolerate higher rates of murder and rape in exchange for apartment buildings untainted by nearby butcher shops?

Good intentions with deadly consequences

Government-mandated safety regulations are often based on faulty infor-mation. If insurance companies or other private organizations realize they have been unwittingly encouraging their clients to engage in risky behav-ior, they will quickly revise their policies. (If they don't, their customers

The Mixed Blessings of Seat Belt Laws

Along with airbag legislation, mandatory seat belt laws present a classic case of unintended con-sequences. For one thing, initial studies that demonstrated large benefits of safety belts may have been misleading, because the type of driver who voluntarily wears a safety belt is likely more cau-tious in general. Most economists believe that driving decisions, just like everything else, are made on the margin. Forcing a driver to wear his seat belt (or to purchase a car with seat belts in the first place) will cause him to be more reckless than he otherwise would be. While few would deny the benefit of wearing a seat belt in the event of a crash—just ask those test dummies—there very well might be more crashes after such legislation.

Sam Peltzman of the University of Chicago has conducted extensive research showing that seat belt and other auto safety regulations have had precisely this impact. His initial findings were that the number of motorist deaths were roughly unchanged—there were more accidents but fewer deaths per accident—yet the total number of deaths from traffic accidents increased, since pedes-trians and bicyclists don't benefit when every driver is forced to wear a seat belt.

Economics Made Simple

The law of unintended consequences: When government attempts to solve a particular problem through coercion, there are inevitably unforeseen side effects. These often make the cure worse than the disease:

- Welfare benefits may encourage out-of-wedlock births and thus increase poverty and crime.

- Rent control may make it difficult for the poor to find decent housing.

- Laws requiring child-resistant packaging for medicine may cause the elderly to store pills in unmarked containers, leading to more overdoses.

- Curfews may reduce the rate of petty crimes but increase violent crimes, as police are diverted and a large number of eyewitnesses are removed from the streets at night.

will switch companies.) But if government regulators impose dangerous practices on the population, they take much longer to admit their mistakes—if they admit them at all. And if they do admit them, it is only to demand more tax dollars so that the mistakes will not happen again. So while businesses are punished if they make a mistake, governmental regulators see their budgets grow with every bureaucrat's mistake.

This tragic fact is illustrated in the history of airbag regulation. Because of airbags' supposed benefits in reducing injuries from collisions, on July 11, 1984, the federal government required that all new vehicles sold in the United States have either driver's side airbags or "automatic seat belts" by the year 1989. In subsequent revisions, all new models were required to have dual front airbags by 1998.

The result was fatal. In low-speed car crashes airbags killed small women and children who otherwise would have survived. In the worst year, 1997, fifty-three fatalities were directly attributed to airbags.

Did the National Highway Traffic Safety Administration (NHTSA) allow airbag installation to be optional, in the interest of protecting small women and children? Of course not. The government believes that airbags save far more lives than they take (a claim, as we'll see, that is open to dispute). So everyone wanting a new car is still required to purchase the devices (which can cost $500 each). However, the gracious NHTSA has a process by which concerned drivers can fill out a form to apply for an exemption. If the NHTSA approves, they will send a letter that the driver can take to a dealer or repair shop who will then install an on/off switch for the airbag. (The airbag cannot be legally removed because it must be turned back on for any occupants of the vehicle who do not meet the NHTSA criteria for exemption.)

At this point, the case of airbags seems to exhibit merely the usual interaction and trade-offs between individual liberty, the community's concern for safety, and bureaucratic stubbornness. The NHTSA's continued claims that airbags save far more lives than they take butts up against the classical liberal argument that people should be free to choose whether their vehicles get airbags. If airbags really are good for most people, then most people will probably choose them voluntarily.

This standoff in the rhetorical dispute received a new twist, however, with a 2005 study by the University of Georgia's Mary Meyer and Tremika Finney. They claimed that even in the general population—not just in the cases of frail women and small children—airbags are harmful and cause more deaths than they prevent. If Meyer and Finney are right, it means that the government has been grossly undercounting the deaths from airbags:

> The National Highway Traffic Safety Administration (NHTSA) keeps track of deaths due to airbags; you can find a list of deaths on the NHTSA website, along with conditions under which these deaths occurred. Each death occurred in a low-speed collision, and for each, there is no other possible cause of death. Is it reasonable to assume that airbags can kill people only at low speeds? Isn't it more likely that airbags also kill people at higher speeds, but the death may be attributed to the crash?

But what of the official statistics that claim airbags have saved thousands of lives? Are Meyer and Finney accusing the government of fabricating data? No, they are not. What they do claim is that the official reports rely on a faulty method: by studying only data taken from crashes in which a fatality occurred, researchers would understandably infer that airbags save lives on net. However, Meyer and Finney ran regressions on data taken from all crashes (whether or not they included a fatality). In this larger pool, they found that airbags cause more harm than good. Meyer and Finney offer the radiation treatment of cancer patients as an analogy:

> [R]adiation treatment will improve their [cancer patients] probability of survival. However, radiation treatment is dangerous and can actually *cause* cancer. Making everyone in the country have airbags and measuring effectiveness only in the fatality group is like making everyone have radiation treatment and looking only at the cancer group to check efficacy. Within the cancer group, radiation will be found to be effective, but there will be more deaths on the whole.
>
> This is what seems to be happening with airbags. In a severe accident, airbags can save lives. However, they are inherently dangerous and pose a risk to the occupant. Our analyses show that in lower-speed crashes, the occupant is significantly more likely to die with an airbag than without.[7]

As the authors explain, it is imperative for researchers to conduct similar studies quickly to verify their findings. This is because government regulations will soon ensure that all vehicles on the road have airbags, and thus statistical assessments of their safety (or danger) will be that much harder. In his classic *On Liberty* John Stuart Mill said that people should be legally free to argue for any viewpoint, no matter how "obviously" false and even reprehensible, in order to protect society from being enslaved to a popular but untrue belief. In the same vein, firms and individuals should have the legal freedom to experiment with different approaches to safety, even ones that most others agree are absurd, because there is always the possibility that the experts and majority opinion are wrong.

Chapter Eight

SETTLING DEBTS

oliticians love to spend money. Even with massive tax payments and control of the printing press, politicians usually
need additional funds to pay for their favorite programs.
When this happens, the politicians—just like any private individual or
company—can borrow money. For example, the government can issue
(sell) a thirty-year Treasury bond, which entitles the bearer to a certain
sum of money from the U.S. Treasury in thirty years' time. (The holder of
the bond also can detach coupons to collect periodic interest payments
from the Treasury.) By selling this bond, the government raises cash in
the present but "goes into debt" by adding a liability against its future revenues. Although the principles are the same here as for any private corporation or individual, the staggering amounts involved foster numerous
myths and fallacies regarding government deficits.

Guess what?

- Deficits don't
cause inflation.
- Deficits don't
stimulate the
economy.
- Tax cuts don't
cause deficits.
- Bill Clinton didn't
really balance the
budget.

Deficits don't cause inflation

By itself, a government budget deficit has no effect on the overall price
level. If the government runs a $300 billion deficit, then yes, the govern-
ment can spend $300 billion more on goods and services, and the sellers
of these items will tend to raise their prices because of the boost in

demand. But where did the $300 billion come from? The government sucked it out of the private sector, meaning households and businesses have $300 billion less to spend. Government borrowing can certainly raise particular prices, but by itself it can't cause general inflation.

Deficits crowd out private investment

Although it doesn't cause inflation, a government deficit is harmful nevertheless because it raises interest rates and "crowds out" private investment. When someone saves money and uses it to buy a Treasury bond, those funds cannot be used to buy, say, a bond from Xerox. In order to raise money for research and development, Xerox (and other companies) must now offer higher rates of return since they are, in effect, competing with the U.S. Treasury to acquire the scarce savings of households. Overall, Xerox and other private companies will end up with less investment because these funds were siphoned off by the government's borrowing.

Most leftists have warned about the danger of government deficits ever since the Reagan administration. But this was not always so. Indeed, in the Keynesian heydays of the 1950s and 1960s, the intelligentsia considered massive deficits an excellent way to prop up "aggregate demand" during a recession. In this way, the wise government overseers thought they could jump-start the ailing economy, which would allegedly stagnate if left to its own devices. The bitter experience of "stagflation" (double-digit unemployment and inflation) during the 1970s convinced most economists that the old Keynesian prescriptions were moonshine.

Raising taxes isn't "responsible"

The liberal media loves to congratulate "mature" and "responsible" politicians for raising taxes, ostensibly to cut the deficit. In contrast, tax cutters (who are usually Republicans) are portrayed as immature and shortsighted demagogues who curry favor with the public by handing out money.

But while government deficits are indeed a problem because they stifle business investment and hence slow economic growth, the solution to this problem is not to increase taxes (which also slows economic growth) but to cut spending! Whenever the government spends a dollar, it sucks real resources away from the private sector (where

Debt versus Deficit

The **deficit** is a "flow concept" that indicates the shortfall between expenditures and revenue during a certain time period. **Debt** is static; it is a stock concept that indicates the total outstanding liabilities at a certain time. Don't expect reporters to know the difference.

they would be used to cater to consumer desires) and devotes them to ends picked by the politicians. From this perspective, it doesn't really matter how the government got the dollar in the first place, whether it was taxed or borrowed. Indeed, if forced to pick between the two financing methods, the method of borrowing is far less coercive and invasive of privacy: because people voluntarily lend money to the government, there is no need for the IRS to pore over their backgrounds.

Burdening our grandchildren?

When lambasting a tax cut, an effective rhetorical device is to remind the public of the burden future generations will supposedly suffer because of today's selfish change in the tax code. These arguments are (mostly) nonsense. If the government returns $100 billion to the taxpayers and increases the deficit by the same amount, it is true that the national debt will be that much higher (plus interest) fifty years down the road. The young workers coming of age will then have more of their tax dollars eaten up every year in making interest payments on the larger debt. But there is another consideration that exactly offsets the first: if the government runs a $100 billion higher deficit today, then future generations will inherit more Treasury bonds than they otherwise would have. After all, to whom will the U.S. Treasury (in fifty years) make these payments? Why, to the grandchildren of the people who today lend the money.

This is not merely semantics or accounting trickery. The rhetoric surrounding tax cuts and budget deficits often makes it sound as if politicians are using time machines to take goodies from future generations so we can selfishly consume them today. Obviously, this is absurd; everything the present generation consumes must be produced out of present resources.

Having said this, there is a real sense in which budget deficits make future generations poorer: a government deficit siphons funds out of the private sector and channels them into pork barrel projects. By lowering private investment, the deficits ensure that future generations inherit a smaller stock of tractors, factories, tools, and other equipment than they otherwise would have. In this sense alone do today's budget deficits impoverish our unborn descendants.

Reagan's record

The favorite example of those hostile to tax cuts is the experience under Reagan. According to the typical version, Ronald Reagan swept into office and enacted irresponsible tax giveaways for the rich. This starved the federal government of revenue and led to unprecedented deficits, which in turn made it difficult for Reagan's successors to increase federal spending because so much was needed just to service the higher debt he bequeathed.

There is just one problem with this standard story: federal tax revenues went way up under Reagan, from $599 billion in 1981 to $991 billion in 1989. The reason for the huge deficits? Federal spending rose even faster than revenues. A case can certainly be made against the fiscal policies of Ronald Reagan, but the deficits of the 1980s were not the fault of tax cuts.

TOTAL FEDERAL OUTLAYS AND RECEIPTS, 1981–1989[1]

Year	Receipts (Millions USD)	Outlays (Millions USD)
1981	599,272	678,241
1982	617,766	745,743
1983	600,562	808,364
1984	666,486	851,853
1985	734,088	946,396
1986	769,215	990,430
1987	854,353	1,004,082
1988	909,303	1,064,455
1989	991,190	1,143,646

Clinton's budget

In contrast to Reagan, Bill Clinton epitomized the modern liberal's idea of responsible fiscal policy: he raised taxes and (apparently) balanced the budget. But here too the story is not so simple. For one thing, in 1997, Clinton (prodded by congressional Republicans) cut the capital gains tax from 28 percent to 20 percent and allowed a much more generous exemption for capital gains on home sales. But second and more to the point, although the official federal budget deficit was indeed eliminated, nevertheless the total federal debt increased every year that Clinton was in office. This discrepancy is possible because of government accounting tricks that would land a private chief financial officer in jail. Bill Clinton's "surpluses" occurred during years in which the government took in more revenues than it paid out in current expenditures. Consequently, the government didn't need to borrow money in those years.

However, this focus on present cash flows leaves out many types of future liabilities, and hence doesn't give a full picture of the government's true financial condition. For an extreme example, if the government decided today that, in the year 2025, anyone forty and older could start collecting Social Security retirement benefits, this change would have tremendous consequences on the solvency of the government. But according to the usual methods, the change wouldn't affect this year's budget deficit. In a similar manner, even though Clinton had a few budget surpluses, nonetheless the government went deeper in debt every year of his time in office.

THE CLINTON YEARS:
FOUR OFFICIAL "SURPLUSES" BUT CONSTANTLY
DEEPER IN OVERALL DEBT[2]

Year	Receipts Minus Outlays (Millions USD)	Gross End of Year Federal Debt (Millions USD)
1998	69,213	5,478,189
1999	125,563	5,605,523
2000	236,445	5,628,700
2001	127,299	5,769,881

The bottom line on debts and deficits is the question of who is more likely to spend your money prudently—you or the government? Answer that, and you'll see why the best strategy for the federal budget is to cut spending *and* taxes.

Chapter Nine

✳✳✳✳✳✳✳✳✳

MONEY AND BANKING

True story: On October 9, 2003, a very large, internationally known manufacturer introduced a new version of one of its most popular products (over 4.5 billion units distributed worldwide). Many smaller clients saw no real reason for the revamped design, but the manufacturer cited security flaws with the earlier model. At first the public seemed eager to snatch up the new product, but market analysts noticed something peculiar: even those who bid the most for the new product soon became unhappy with it and consequently sold or gave it to someone else, sometimes a mere few hours after purchase. Like the proverbial fruitcake during the holiday season, millions of people kept passing along the product to family, friends, or even total strangers, who in turn wouldn't keep it for very long. The strangest thing of all, however, was that these same people—like clockwork—would very soon go out and buy *more* of the item, but then quickly turn around and dump it.

I am not referring to mass delusion over a gimmicky invention but rather to a quite familiar product: the U.S. Treasury's $20 bill. Because all of us have grown up in a monetary economy, its practices do not strike as us odd. Yet if we ponder the nature of money itself, it is indeed quite peculiar. In its modern form, money isn't really useful for anything; you can't eat it, and little pictures of presidents on green pieces of paper aren't

Guess what?

🏦 Money was created by capitalism, not by government.

🏦 Governments, not greed, cause inflation.

🏦 The gold standard would work in today's economy.

🏦 Free market banks are safer than government-regulated ones.

particularly good for building anything. Even so, people destroy marriages and murder each other trying to get their hands on as much of the stuff as possible.

Unfortunately, the study of money, and its related field, banking, is rife with quacks and cranks. Hundreds of influential writers and theorists—not to mention politicians—have bamboozled the public with crazy schemes that promise untold prosperity and claim to have no strings attached. In this chapter we'll debunk some of these myths and gain a basic understanding of money and banking.

Barter is barbarous

Leftists and moralists take delight in denigrating money, but the simple fact is that money makes modern civilization possible. A world without money would not be a utopia; it would be a nightmare in which most of the earth's current population would starve to death. Money is a tool of tremendous importance that helps bring order to the inconceivably complicated flow of resources and products around the globe. In this role,

Learning FDR's Style at the School of Hard Knox

Everyone knows of the huge gold depository at Fort Knox, Kentucky. What most people don't know is that it was built to store all the gold that the federal government forcibly removed from the general public. After all, when you take away the country's stock of money, you have to put it somewhere! At its peak, during World War II, Fort Knox reportedly held over 18,000 tons of gold—enough to make ninety solid-gold Statues of Liberty.

money is as crucial as the mathematics behind it.

To get a glimpse of the service money provides, we should try to imagine life without it. For a simple but illustrative example, consider a dentist. In a monetary economy he sells his professional services to a wide range of clients whose only common bond is that they all suffer toothaches, need

A Book You're Not Supposed to Read

Money Mischief: Episodes in Monetary History by Milton Friedman; New York: Harcourt Brace Jovanovich, 1992.

braces, and so on. The dentist provides his services in exchange for money, and then uses this money to buy the things he wants: apples, sweaters, a new CD, or someone to clean his gutters once a year.

If it weren't for money, the dentist couldn't separate his sales and purchases in this fashion. Rather than selling his services to anyone with the proper number of dollar bills, he would instead have to find people with apples who also had toothaches, people with sweaters who also wanted braces, people with CDs who also wanted cleanings, and so forth. This would severely limit the range of trades. But it gets worse: even if the dentist found someone who had sweaters that the dentist liked and who also wanted to get braces, this wouldn't be enough. It would be worth the dentist's efforts to treat him only if he were willing to trade a very large number of sweaters. They might agree to a complicated plan in which the dentist would install braces and then receive scores of sweaters over the coming years, but this too would be cumbersome and would greatly limit the scope of trading.

The dentist could take 144 sweaters in exchange for a root canal, and then plan to trade his surplus sweaters for other goods or services. But now he would be forced to become both a dentist and a sweater salesman, even if the latter were neither his expertise nor his calling.

As this fanciful example illustrates, a world without money would be a miserable one. Rather than our current system of division of labor, in which people specialize in particular occupations and thus raise total output, people would have to be largely self-sufficient. We'd all grow our own food, make our own clothing, and build our own tools. Trade is still possible in a world without money, but most potentially beneficial trades would remain unfulfilled because of coordination problems.

Nobody invented money

Like language and science, nobody invented money. There was no wise king who perceived the drawbacks to pure barter and so ordered his subjects to adopt a single item that would constitute one side of every transaction. For one thing, it would take a rare genius to see the possibilities of money without having experienced it; in a world of barter, someone talking about the switch to money would sound crazy. ("Instead of trading away your valuable pigs for horses, why not accept some smooth stones? Don't worry that you don't want them; someone else will give you those horses in exchange for the stones! C'mon, everybody, if we could all just agree that these useless stones are valuable, we'd all be so much better off!") Another problem with the "state" theory of the origin of money is that there is no historical record of any such wise ruler, even though we have ample evidence that ancient civilizations used money.

As with the capitalist economy itself, the development of money was an unintended but hugely serendipitous byproduct of merchants' selfish behavior. Carl Menger, the founder of the so-called Austrian school of economics, offered a convincing sketch way back in the late 1800s of how money must

---

✛✛✛✛✛✛✛✛

I'll Give You Two Slices for That Sweater: Objects Used as Money throughout History

Bread	Cigarettes
Shells	Red ochre
Salt	Rum
Iron nails	Whales' teeth

have developed. Menger first noted that even in a state of pure barter, some items are more marketable, or "liquid," than others. For example, a farmer bringing his cows to town will find more buyers than a manufacturer bringing a new telescope that he hopes to trade for some chickens and butter. Because of this difference, traders with particularly unmarketable ("illiquid") items might not find anyone who wanted their wares *and* wished to exchange the very items that the traders wanted. A second best procedure, Menger argued, would be to trade away the unmarketable items for things that were more marketable—in the hopes that these newly acquired items could then in turn be used to trade for the objects ultimately desired. To return to our example, the owner of the telescope might trade it to a blacksmith in exchange for some tools, which then could be traded to a farmer for the chickens and butter.

The "Full Faith and Credit" of the U.S. Government?

When discussing the difference between a gold standard and fiat currency, people often say that U.S. dollars are now "backed up" by the government itself. Strictly speaking, this is nonsense; under a fiat standard, nothing backs up the paper money. The green pieces of paper in one's wallet today represent no obligation whatsoever on the U.S. government. Furthermore, the government doesn't really dictate the purchasing power of money, except in the sense that it controls how many dollar bills there are, and people's willingness to hold money is fairly stable. But if everyone in the world suddenly decided that former presidents were so ugly that they didn't want to carry around pictures of them, prices (quoted in U.S. dollars) would go through the roof and the government would have no way to control this. Even in a monopolized market, the forces of supply and demand ultimately set prices.

A Book You're Not Supposed to Read

What Has Government Done to Our Money? by Murray Rothbard; Auburn, AL: Ludwig von Mises Institute, 2005.

Menger pointed out that this process would snowball over time. Those items that initially enjoyed a large market, even in pure barter, would become even more liquid, as more and more people would accept them in trade simply because they were acceptable by so many other people. Eventually, one or two goods would outstrip all others in their acceptability in trade, and thus would become *money*. As capitalism developed, precious metals filled this role, although historically all sorts of different commodities have served as money. The important point is that money emerged spontaneously on the market, and the original types of money were all useful commodities that were initially valued for their own intrinsic properties.

We're from the government and we're here to help

Naturally, kings and other rulers couldn't leave well enough alone, and have always sought involvement in matters of money. Under the guise of preventing fraud and ensuring a standard framework, governments have largely monopolized control of the money supply, even though the production and distribution of money was formerly handled on the market—just as the production and distribution of automobiles is currently handled without government management.

The movement from commodity-based money such as gold and silver to "fiat currency" based on intrinsically useless pieces of paper was a slow one. In the United States, the dollar could originally be exchanged for a specified weight of gold and/or silver. That's why the public initially accepted the notes—they were essentially tickets that could be turned in for the "real" money. Over time, people grew accustomed to thinking of the paper as money, and no revolution ensued when in 1933 FDR reneged on the government's contractual obligations to redeem notes in gold. He even forced U.S. citizens to turn in their stocks of gold in exchange for pieces of paper. In 1971, Richard Nixon finally severed the last formal link between the U.S. dollar and gold, so that even foreign central banks (let alone private U.S. citizens) couldn't exchange their fiat dollars for a good that was actually useful.

Printing more money makes prices rise

Most intellectuals look down their nose on "gold bugs," thinking them Neanderthal reactionaries who don't understand "progress." The gold standard is reviled because of its apparent absurdity: Why hire men and machines to dig up gold from a mine only to bury it again in a bank vault? Wouldn't the whole system be much more sensible if we allowed a large margin for "pretend" money, in which there are more dollars in circulation than the government can back up with gold—or better yet, to not tie dollars to anything at all?

What these modern scientific types overlook is the basic fact that the gold standard forced responsibility on the politicians. When the government is legally obliged to turn over a specific amount of gold to anyone who turns in paper dollars, it can't run the printing press willy-nilly. On the other hand, with fiat money the only costs of printing more dollars are the materials used in the process. As any private counterfeiter can attest, it's definitely a profitable venture to buy ink and paper and use it to print crisp $100 bills.

Although the U.S. experience has been far better than that of other countries, even here

Economics Made Simple

fiat currency: A type of currency (usually paper money) whose value is derived from a government mandate. Unlike commodity or representative money, it is not based in a valued commodity, such as gold or silver, and is not covered by a special reserve. Fiat money holds its value as long as its holders feel that they can find an exchange partner for it in the future.

the dangerous plan of letting politicians play with the printing press has yielded predictably poor results. According to Milton Friedman:

> All told, in the United States, prices in 1990 were fifteen times their initial level in 1891; in Britain, fifty times.... The rate of inflation during the first half of the century (1891–1940) averaged under 1 percent a year in the United States, 1.6 percent in Britain. During the second half it quadrupled in both countries, averaging 4 percent in the United States, 6.4 percent in Britain.[1]

The government is always quick to transfer the blame for inflation onto someone else; unions, greedy businessmen, and Arab oil tycoons are all suitable scapegoats. Yet these groups can at best raise particular prices, not prices in general. If Americans have to spend more on gasoline, that leaves less money to spend on burgers and sneakers. In order to raise prices in general, the government must print more money. As Friedman and other economists have documented in countries from Brazil to interwar Germany to Soviet Russia, and from different time periods going back to ancient China, price inflation is always and everywhere a monetary phenomenon.

Banking basics

Although banking is a complicated and intimidating topic, the fundamentals are simple. Banks serve two basic purposes. First, they are warehouses; rather than keeping stockpiles of money (whether gold or paper currency) lying around the house, most people prefer the security of a bank vault. The second and subtler function of banks is to act as credit intermediaries, or middlemen between lenders and borrowers.

Because of our current fractional reserve system, in which banks can lend out more money than they have on deposit in the vaults, the line between the two functions is blurry. Most people now earn an interest return even on checking accounts; it seems as if the bank is paying to store money that in theory the customer is still able to spend at a moment's notice.

In contrast, under a 100 percent reserve system the two functions would be quite distinct. If a depositor wanted to be able to write checks on his funds, he would open a checking account and would have to actually pay the bank a small fee for guarding his assets. On the other hand, if a depositor wished to earn interest, he would open a true savings account, and wouldn't be able to touch the money for a contractually specified period. The money put into the savings account would no longer be his, as it would have been transferred to the checking accounts of home buyers and others who borrowed from the bank (at higher interest rates). With procedures such as these, banking would still be a viable enterprise even if the sum total of all customers' checkbook balances were backed up 100 percent by money in the vaults.

Hyperinflation: How to Drive People to Hitler

We Americans are upset when prices rise more than 4 percent in a given year, and are scandalized at double-digit increases. In interwar Germany, the wholesale price index rose from 100.6 in July 1922 to 194,000 in July 1923—a shocking inflation rate exceeding 190,000 percent. By November 1923, the price index was a ludicrous 726 billion—an inflation rate of roughly 4,300 percent per month. By the end of 1923, 150 printing companies had two thousand presses operating around the clock churning out new paper money. Workers would be paid up to three times per day, and their wives would take the wages—in suitcases and, according to some, even wheelbarrows—and rush to trade them for any tangible good they could find.[2]

"Wildcat" banking

From 1837 to 1861, the federal government left bank regulation up to the individual states. This period of relatively free banking is often viewed as a chaotic wasteland in which individuals could open up a bank and start issuing currency just as easily as they could open up a restaurant and start serving food. The frequent bank collapses and financial panics supposedly proved that unregulated banking was foolhardy.

As with so many other historical justifications of government intervention, this one is largely a myth. For one thing, the era of so-called free banking was hardly laissez-faire; the state governments set numerous regulations, and moreover these regulations may have encouraged the very problems at issue. Second, it is by no means clear why the panics of the 1800s were worse than the Great Depression and rampant price inflation of the 1900s.

How could state regulations make the banking system more precarious? Well, because, as economists George Selgin and Larry White explain, "they required banks to collateralize their notes by lodging specified assets (usually state government bonds) with state authorities."[3] Why did that matter? Because later on, "clusters of 'free bank' failures were principally due to falling prices of the state bonds they held, suggesting that the bond-collateral requirements caused bank portfolios to become overloaded with state bonds."[4] In other words, government regulation actually unbalanced the banking system.

More generally, we must ask ourselves, how are bank runs possible? Clearly, under a 100 percent reserve system, banks would never fail in this way. Investors wouldn't worry about getting their money back, just as customers of dry cleaners don't have widespread anxiety attacks

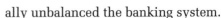

A Book You're Not Supposed to Read

The Rationale of Central Banking and the Free Banking Alternative by Vera Smith; New York: Liberty Press, 1990.

and rush to retrieve their garments. By shielding banks from their contractual obligations, government policies encourage recklessness. (Although it happened after the so-called free banking era, the famous "bank holiday" proclaimed by FDR—closing the banks for several days to "cool off" bank runs—is a prime example.) State regulations that limited branch banking also lent support to fly-by-night organizations. How? Because by keeping reputable, solid banks from sweeping the country, the government ensured that residents in rural areas had fewer banking choices and might have to patronize less stable banks.

Ironically, runs on banks and other "panics" were the very mechanisms to keep the bankers honest. In a truly competitive market, if Joe Smith opens a bank, he can't force anybody to hold Smith Notes or force any merchants to accept them at their stores. The only way for Joe Smith to convince the public to accept his bank notes is to pledge to redeem them for a specified amount of gold (or other valued commodity). Assuming he can get his operation off the ground, what is to prevent Smith (and other private bankers) from printing up more notes than he can actually redeem?

One way is to trust government regulators to design an honest system and run it responsibly. Another, less naïve, way is to let banks go out of business when they default on promises to their customers. Bankers are grown-ups; they can take it. If they know they'll be held liable for their decisions, bankers will be more careful with their funds. A bank that is deemed "too big to fail"—meaning it will get billions in government bailouts if its investments turn sour—is a bank that takes too many risks.

Chapter Ten

GROWING PAINS

Perhaps the single biggest myth underlying the public's support for governmental regulation of business is that pure capitalism led to the Great Depression. In this typical view—propagated every year in state-approved history texts—the 1920s were an era of unrestrained laissez-faire. The wild stock market allowed massive margin buying that caused, or at least exacerbated, the crash on Black Friday. Rising unemployment made consumers fearful, so they curtailed their spending; businesses in turn saw their sales plummet and laid off workers. This vicious cycle continued in a downward spiral, and the market was unable to rescue itself. It took the wise leadership of Franklin Roosevelt, and ultimately World War II, to pull the United States out of the hole that the free market had dug for itself. A classic illustration of the alleged monstrosities of unrestricted capitalism occurs in *The Grapes of Wrath*, when starving but honest folk watch helplessly as oranges are intentionally doused with kerosene in order to decrease supply and thus raise prices.

You, dear reader, will not be surprised to hear that every element of this official tale is dead wrong. First, the Federal Reserve, not pure capitalism, caused the Great Depression. Second, this government mismanagement occurred during the 1920s, which were far from an era of

Guess what?

- 🏠 The business cycle is a product of government, not the free market.

- 🏠 Herbert Hoover didn't practice laissez-faire.

- 🏠 FDR made the Depression worse.

- 🏠 Soviet "growth" was phony and inefficient.

laissez-faire. Third, the New Deal made the Depression worse. (Hint: who do you think ordered the intentional destruction of crops?) And fourth, wars don't make countries richer. In this chapter we'll explore each of these points, as well as other fallacies concerning economic growth.

The business cycle: Courtesy of the government

Every year, some businesses thrive while others fail. In the normal operation of the market, successful entrepreneurs are rewarded with profits and growth, while unsuccessful businesses are penalized by losses and ultimately bankruptcy. Yet when we speak of the business cycle, we refer to the periodic rise and fall of business fortunes in general. The question isn't, "Why do some businesses need to lay off workers and scale back operations?" Rather, it is, "Why is it that sometimes *most* businesses realize their prior forecasts were overly optimistic?"

One view—held by theoretical Marxists as well as by laymen—holds that the business cycle is a natural outcome of the capitalist system. The problem with this explanation is that there is nothing to distinguish booms from busts. If free enterprise causes depressions, why did the worst one happen in the 1930s, rather than, say, the 1850s or the 1880s? Certainly the American market was just as "wildcat" in those earlier decades.

A different view holds that government intervention in the monetary and banking system causes the business cycle. Within this broad category we can distinguish between the monetarist theory, as exemplified by Milton Friedman, versus the Austrian theory, as developed by Ludwig von Mises and Friedrich Hayek. Although this book is not the place to evaluate the merits and weaknesses of these rival interpretations, a brief summary will underscore the claim that the Great Depression (and business cycles in general) was not the fault of the free market.

The monetarist view (explained for the layman in Friedman's *Capitalism and Freedom*) holds that the government ought to maintain a slow

USSR: "Starving to Greatness"

"[T]he excellence, from a technological point of view, of some parts of the Russian industrial equipment, which most strikes the casual observer and which is commonly regarded as evidence of success, has little significance in so far as the answer to the central question [of economic efficiency] is concerned. Whether the new plant will prove to be a useful link in the industrial structure for increasing output depends not only on technological considerations, but even more on the general economic situation. The best tractor factory may not be an asset, and the capital invested in it is a sheer loss, if the labour which the tractor replaces is cheaper than the cost of the material and labour, which goes to make a tractor, plus interest."

Friedrich Hayek, "The Present State of the Debate," in *Collectivist Economic Planning* (1937)

and constant growth in the money supply. Such predictability would reassure the financial markets and lead to smoother, steadier growth in real output. In contrast, the actual policies of the Federal Reserve almost defy belief. In the panicky three years after the great crash in 1929, the Fed responded by cutting the money supply by almost one-third! Is it any wonder, according to Friedmanites, that this general downturn was deeper and more prolonged than previous ones in U.S. history?

The Austrian theory of the trade cycle places the blame on the existence of a central banking and monetary authority itself. Many Austrians believe that in a truly free market, the money supply would consist of a hard commodity such as gold or silver, and banks would have 100 percent reserves. With government privileges—and particularly with the establishment of the Fed—however, the nation's banks were effectively organized into a giant cartel, in which the official money supply could expand faster than the actual reserves in the vaults. In brief, the Austrian theory holds that the boom of the 1920s was largely illusory, built on phantom credit without the real savings and investment necessary to fulfill all the business plans. At some point reality had to reassert itself—the crash and bust—and the economy needed time to liquidate the "malinvestments" made during the period of artificial prosperity. FDR's policies, of course, only prolonged and hampered the readjustment process, where labor and other resources needed to be reallocated to their best uses.

One personal anecdote wonderfully illustrates the obvious flaw in the conventional history: one of my students, while doing an internship in Washington, visited the Federal Reserve. During the tour, he saw an exhibit that listed major dates in the Fed's history. It listed the Federal Reserve Act of 1913, the official start of the federal reserve system in 1914, and major events such as the world wars and the tenures of various chairmen. However, a surprising omission from the timeline was the Great Depression. My bewildered student asked the tour guide about this, and later was told that the exhibit's creators must not have felt that was an important event to include. Indeed, whenever someone asserts that government oversight is necessary to prevent another depression, the

Economic History Made Simple

The Smoot-Hawley Tariff Act of 1930 raised U.S. tariffs to historically high levels. The point was to protect farmers from foreign agricultural imports, but once the tariff revision process got started, it proved impossible to stop. Calls for increased protection flooded in from industrial special-interest groups and soon a bill meant for farmers was raising tariffs in all sectors of the economy. It provoked a storm of retaliatory measures, and is widely credited with exacerbating the Great Depression.

cynic should ask, "Then why didn't the Federal Reserve prevent the first one, since by that point it had been in operation for fifteen years?"

The "progressive" Herbert Hoover

In order for the official myths sanctifying FDR to make any sense, the president before him—Herbert Hoover—must be cast as a do-nothing reactionary, whose reluctance to interfere with the free market persisted even after the onset of the Great Depression. Indeed, this is what most Americans have been taught. Yet this too is complete balderdash. Not only did the government create—or at least exacerbate— the Depression with its unsound monetary policies, but the Hoover administration also deviated from the relatively laissez-faire responses of previous presidents to earlier cyclical downturns.

As comprehensively documented by Murray Rothbard, Herbert Hoover's career in government revealed his interventionist streak as early as 1921, when Harding appointed him secretary of commerce. Hoover wished to transform the Department of Commerce into "the economic interpreter to the American people" because they "badly need one." Upon assuming his post, Hoover quickly established a committee on unemployment to deal with the lingering problems of the 1920–1921 depression.[1] In his own words:

> We developed cooperation between the federal, state, and municipal governments to increase public works. We persuaded employers to "divide" time among their employees so that as many as possible would have some incomes. We organized the industries to undertake renovation, repair, and, where possible, expand construction.[2]

A few years later, in 1926, Secretary Hoover (now under President Coolidge) boasted of the "new economics" and its method for overturning the business cycle:

> [N]ot so many years ago the employer considered it was in his interest to use the opportunities of unemployment and immigration to lower wages irrespective of other considerations. The lowest wages and longest hours were then conceived as the means to obtain lowest production costs and largest profits.....But we are a long way on the road to new conceptions. The very essence of great production is high wages and low prices, because it depends upon a widening...consumption, only to be obtained from the purchasing-power of high real wages and increased standards of living.[3]

As with FDR after him, Herbert Hoover's efforts (whether through jawboning or more explicit measures) to maintain wage rates in the midst of massive unemployment was a perfect recipe for prolonging the Great Depression. Whereas the American economy had purged itself of previous depressions generally within a year or two, the Great Depression lingered partly because wages were held above their natural market-clearing levels. Workers could not be rearranged in light of the new circumstances because the primary method of coordination—the signals provided by accurate market prices and wages—was thwarted by Hoover and later by FDR. At the urging of President Hoover, big business—including the telephone, steel, and automobile industries—agreed to maintain real wages and cooperate with each other to weather the downturn. Even the American Federation of Labor applauded the Hoover administration's response to the Depression. In its journal, the AFL editorialized in 1930 that:

> The President's conference has given industrial leaders a new sense of their responsibilities....Never before have they been

called upon to act together . . . in earlier recessions they have acted individually to protect their own interests and . . . have intensified depressions.[4]

In addition to preventing wage adjustment, the Hoover administration proposed massive increases in state and federal public works programs. The administration also increased farm subsidies and urged farmers to reduce their acreage (and hence "support" farm prices). In 1930 Hoover signed the crippling Smoot-Hawley tariff against the advice of most of the nation's economists and large bankers. Also in that year, Hoover helped "mitigate" the unemployment figure by restricting immigration to all but the wealthiest immigrants; his policy change reduced the influx of European newcomers by 90 percent within a few months.

A Book You're Not Supposed to Read

FDR's Folly: How Roosevelt and His New Deal Prolonged the Great Depression by Jim Powell; New York: Crown Forum, 2003.

In light of the above examples, it is clear that Herbert Hoover was not the "friend of big business" and proponent of laissez-faire that most history books claim. What is the source of this myth? Is it that Hoover sold himself as a believer in property rights and economic liberty to the voters, and that future historians were hoodwinked by his campaign rhetoric? Perhaps, but the following description of Hoover's response to the 1929 crash by Hoover himself during his bid for reelection suggests otherwise:

[W]e might have done nothing. That would have been utter ruin. Instead we met the situation with proposals to private business and to Congress of the most gigantic program of economic defense and counterattack ever evolved in the history of the Republic. We put it into action. . . . No government in Washington has hitherto considered that it held so broad a responsibility for leadership in such times. . . . For the first time in the history of depression, dividends, profits, and the cost of living, have been reduced before wages have suffered. . . . They were maintained until the cost of living had decreased and the profits had practically vanished. They are now the highest real wages in the world.

Creating new jobs and giving to the whole system a new breath of life; nothing has ever been devised in our history which has done more for . . . "the common run of men and women." . . . Some of the reactionary economists urged that we should allow the liquidation to take its course until we had found bottom. . . . We determined that we would not follow the advice of the bitter-end liquidationists and see the whole body of debtors of the United States brought to bankruptcy and the savings of our people brought to destruction.[5]

In another odd twist, Hoover's opponent, Franklin Delano Roosevelt, accused Hoover of "reckless and extravagant" spending, of thinking that "we ought to center control of everything in Washington as rapidly as possible," and of leading the "greatest spending administration in peacetime in all of history."[6]

The New Deal didn't fix the Depression

Hoover's interference with the market prolonged the Depression, and FDR's New Deal policies—which were simply expansions of the "bold" Hoover innovations—only made matters worse, by postponing the liquidation of unsound projects and the quick return to normalcy that had characterized all previous depressions. On this point there can be little arguing with the historical facts: when FDR's "First 100 Days" of intense legislation began in 1933, unemployment was a staggering 24.9 percent.

Despite (or because of) the unprecedented New Deal measures, unemployment fell slowly over the next four years, and was "only" 14.3 percent by 1937. (To repeat, earlier American depressions were over within two years.) Yet in 1938, unemployment shot up again to 19 percent. In what possible sense, then, did the New Deal "cure" the Great Depression?

One of the most celebrated aspects of the New Deal was the National Recovery Administration (NRA)—here was the epitome of "scientific" planning, as opposed to blind reliance on autonomous market forces. Yet according to economist Larry Reed, the NRA (often dubbed the "National Run Around" by its critics) erected a system of "government-mandated cartels" in a "fascist-style arrangement." But despite the erosions of

Roosevelt's Jack-Booted Thugs

When it wasn't busy ordering farmers to plow under fields (in order to reduce crop supplies and thus boost farm prices), the Roosevelt administration was micromanaging output and pricing decisions through the NRA codes. John T. Flynn describes the methods Roosevelt's "saviors of capitalism" used to enforce these regulations:

> The NRA was discovering it could not enforce its rules. Black markets grew up. Only the most violent police methods could procure enforcement. In Sidney Hillman's garment industry the code authority employed enforcement police. They roamed through the garment district like storm troopers. They could enter a man's factory, send him out, line up his employees, subject them to minute interrogation, take over his books on the instant. Night work was forbidden. Flying squadrons of these private coat-and-suit police went through the district at night, battering down doors with axes looking for men who were committing the crime of sewing together a pair of pants at night. But without these harsh methods many code authorities said there could be no compliance because the public was not back of it.[7]

Don't Hold Your Breath

"I confidently predict the collapse of capitalism and the beginning of history. Something will go wrong in the machinery that converts money into money, the banking system will collapse totally, and we will be left having to barter to stay alive. Those who can dig in their garden will have a better chance than the rest. I'll be all right; I've got a few veg."

Margaret Drabble,
Guardian, January 2, 1993

traditional liberty, did the NRA at least get the economy running again? Here is Reed's answer:

The economic impact of the NRA was immediate and powerful. In the five months leading up to the act's passage, signs of recovery were evident: factory employment and payrolls had increased by 23 and 35 percent, respectively. Then came the NRA, shortening hours of work, raising wages arbitrarily, and imposing other new costs on enterprise. In the six months after the law took effect, industrial production dropped 25 percent. [Economist] Benjamin M. Anderson writes, "NRA was not a revival measure. It was an antirevival measure.... Through the whole of the NRA period industrial production did not rise as high as it had been in July 1933, before NRA came in."[8]

Did World War II get us out of the Depression?

Many Americans, correctly skeptical of the claim that Roosevelt's New Deal rescued the U.S. from the Depression, offer the alternative theory that World War II jump-started the economy. Yet this explanation makes little sense. After all, wars devour resources and kill millions of workers; how could they possibly be good for economic growth?

Henry Hazlitt (following nineteenth-century economist Frédéric Bastiat) dubbed this mistake the "broken window fallacy." Besides crediting wars with growth, the fallacy rears its ugly head every time some commentator remarks that a hurricane or earthquake will "stimulate output" because of the necessary rebuilding efforts. Hazlitt pointed out the absurdity in this view: when workers and other resources are used to simply repair or replace damaged items, no new wealth is created. Were it not for the hurricane (or explosives from enemy bombers), the workers and other resources could have been used to enlarge the existing stocks of capital and consumption goods.

The broken window fallacy is easy to avoid once recognized. But unfortunately, the typical statistics used by mainstream economists reinforce bad habits of thought. Sending millions of productive young men to fight and die overseas, as well as diverting massive quantities of raw

The Broken Window

"This little act of vandalism will in the first instance mean more business for a glazier. The glazier will be no more unhappy to learn of the incident than an undertaker to learn of a death. But the shopkeeper will be out the $250 that he was planning to spend on a new suit. Because he has had to replace a window, he will have to go without the suit (or some equivalent need or luxury). Instead of having a window and $250 he now has merely a window. Or, as he was planning to buy the suit that very afternoon, instead of having both a window and a suit he must be content with the window and no suit. If we think of him as a part of the community, the community has lost a new suit that might otherwise have come into being, and is just that much poorer. The glazier's gain of business, in short, is merely the tailor's loss of business. No new 'employment' has been added."

Henry Hazlitt, *Economics in One Lesson*

materials into the war effort, could only make Americans poorer. (Of course, many would argue that the price was worth it—but the point is that it was costly to enter World War II.) Nonetheless, this price tag was masked by the official measurements of gross domestic product used to gauge an economy's performance. In the next section we'll see the problems with this approach.

The whole is not the sum of the parts

As is so often the case, one of the biggest problems in the public's understanding of economic growth is the faulty statistics trumpeted by mainstream economists and parroted by politicians and the press. The single most important number in assessing the overall strength of the economy is the Gross Domestic Product (GDP), which measures the total market value of all finished goods and services produced within the United States. (Economists used to use Gross National Product [GNP], which measures the value of final output produced by all citizens, regardless of their location. This difference is relatively unimportant for our purposes.) The typical measure of growth is then the annual percentage increase in GDP, after adjusting for inflation. As we shall see, using GDP figures as a basis for economic policy is a dangerous practice indeed, and ironically stifles true growth.

A Book You're Not Supposed to Read

The Roosevelt Myth by John T. Flynn; San Francisco: Fox & Wilkes, 1998.

The textbooks acknowledge some of the obvious drawbacks to their figure. A classic (and politically incorrect!) example is the case of a man who marries his housekeeper. Before their marriage, her services (laundry, vacuuming, cooking) were bought in the open market and thus contributed to official GDP. But after marrying, the new housewife performs these identical tasks for "free," and hence official GDP drops by her pre-

How to Whip Inflation: Kill the Fed

"What, then, should the government do if the Austrian theory is the correct one?…It can only cure the chronic and potentially runaway inflation in one way: by ceasing to inflate; by stopping its own expansion of the money supply by Federal Reserve manipulation, either by lowering reserve requirements or by purchasing assets in the open market. The fault of inflation is not in business 'monopoly,' or in union agitation, or in the hunches of speculators, or in the 'greediness' of consumers; the fault is in the legalized counterfeiting operations of the government itself. For the government is the only institution in society with the power to counterfeit—to create new money. So long as it continues to use that power, we will continue to suffer from inflation, even unto a runaway inflation that will utterly destroy the currency. At the very least, we must call upon the government to stop using that power to inflate. But since all power possessed will be used and abused, a far sounder method of ending inflation would be to deprive the government completely of the power to counterfeit: either by passing a law forbidding the Fed to purchase any further assets or to lower reserve requirements, or more fundamentally, to abolish the Federal Reserve System altogether."

Murray Rothbard, *America's Great Depression*

vious annual salary. Likewise, black market operations by their very nature go unreported to government statisticians, and hence escape inclusion in the official GDP figures.

Although these drawbacks are serious enough—indeed, as economist Pete Boettke argues, in communist countries black market transactions allow the enslaved people to survive!—they deflect attention from the real problems with the official measure: the official GDP figure completely excludes all "intermediate" expenditures. Consequently, it downplays the importance of the capitalists, and exaggerates the role of final consumers and government expenditures. Economist Mark Skousen explains:

> GNP takes into account only the production of goods and services sold to final users. It excludes all economic activity associated with the production of intermediate inputs, that is, raw materials, semimanufactured goods, wholesale goods, and other unfinished products (including inventories) that have yet to reach the final consumption stage. GNP includes . . . the purchase of all new durable capital goods, such as machines and equipment, because they are treated as final products. But these goods do not include nondurable capital goods or intermediate products such as leather or steel. In short, GNP takes into account fixed capital but not circulating capital. Thus, GNP is not really a gross figure at all, but a net value-added approach.[9]

The reason mainstream economists omit these intermediate products is to avoid "double counting." They argue that, for example, to count the total expenditures on the flour and oats that go into the production of a loaf of bread would be to exaggerate output. Even so, their preferred solution—to net out these gross expenditures at each stage and count only the "value added"—underlies gross errors of policy. Skousen continues:

A Book You're Not Supposed to Read

Economics on Trial: Lies, Myths, and Realites by Mark Skousen; Scarborough, Ontario: Irwin, 1990.

Because they leave out intermediate goods, GNP data grossly [exaggerate] the level of consumption in the economy. . . . [A]ccording to national income statistics, consumption represented 66 percent of GNP in 1988. . . . Naturally, this high level implies that the U.S. economy is consumer-oriented, that changes in consumer spending—not investment or business spending—are the key to economic growth or decline. In fact, according to GNP data, government spending is more important than private investment ($936 billion for government purchases versus $765 [billion] for private domestic investment). The overemphasis on consumption is a common misconception found in the financial press and economic commentaries. Especially during the Christmas holidays, the media report almost daily on the outlook for retail sales, suggesting that if holiday sales are up the economy is healthy and sound. Underlying these reports is the notion that if only the Christmas season lasted year-round, the economy could expand even more.[10]

To recap: by netting out gross business expenditures at each stage of production in order to isolate the "value added," the conventional GDP (or GNP) exaggerates the relative importance of spending—both by consumers and by the government. To put it another way, using data from Skousen: In 2005 personal consumption expenditures (roughly $8.7 trillion) were 70 percent of GNP (roughly $12.5 trillion); such a percentage seems to back up the hoopla over "consumer confidence" and "retail spending" figures. In contrast, official net private investment was a paltry $2.1 trillion, a mere 16.8 percent of GNP. However, this number in no way captures the total amount of spending by private businesses, for it has netted out (as "double counting") $14.6 trillion in other gross investment by businesses, on things such as raw materials, supplies, and additions to inventories. After adding this spending to both the total figure and to the business sector, we find that consumer expenditures represented only 32 percent of total economic activity in 2005, while business spending accounted for 62 percent of the augmented figure.[11]

Economic Growth Isn't Inflationary

It is simply taken for granted among financial commentators in the media that increased output causes price inflation. This Keynesian mindset was crystallized in the famous Phillips Curve, which graphically depicted the alleged tradeoff between unemployment and inflation. The idea was that "easy" monetary and budget policies would cure recession but at the cost of rising prices, while tight policies would nip inflation in the bud all right, but would also cause massive layoffs.

This analysis works neither in theory nor practice. First, the theory: If you think about it for a moment, it is obvious that increased real output will lower the money price per unit of output. After all, inflation occurs when too much money chases too few goods. Second, the practice: There are countless examples of high inflation and low output (e.g. the U.S. in the 1970s) or low inflation and growing output (e.g. the U.S. in the 1980s).

A (government) penny spent is a penny earned

Besides the problems mentioned above, there is a more fundamental flaw with the popular macroeconomic figures: they treat money spent by the government as output. To understand this strange viewpoint, we need to review the conventional approach to measuring economic activity.

Suppose we want to measure how much output the Smith household produces. One way is to count up how much income the Smiths earn from various sources. For example, if Mr. Smith makes $10,000 per year in public talks and $90,000 as a college professor, while Mrs. Smith makes $20,000 writing short stories and $30,000 selling beauty products, then the Smith household produces $150,000 worth of output annually.

Another way of arriving at this same figure, of course, would be to sum up how much others spend on the Smiths' services. Thus there are two approaches to computing aggregate output: measuring income or measuring expenditures.

This explains the typical approach to GDP calculation. When someone buys a new car, this increases the official GDP statistics for the year. Despite the obvious objection to this approach—after all, handing over dollar bills for something isn't itself productive—there is a certain plausibility to it. What we're really measuring isn't the productivity of the consumer, but rather the productivity of the car producer, and the only yardstick of economic value we have is how much consumers voluntarily spend on goods and services.

Fair enough, at least when it comes to things paid for by private individuals and firms. But is this process at all sensible when it comes to government expenditures? Not really. Consider the notorious case, uncovered in a 1983 audit, of the Pentagon spending $600 each on toilet seats. Should these government expenditures really have gone into the total output for the U.S. economy? Clearly not. At best, the normal market price of toilet seats should have been used, because when the government pays for something—in contrast to a private individual or corporation—there is no assurance that the price really reflects the underlying value of the item.

The difference is due to the simple fact that government ultimately gets its money through taxation or the printing press, and so its "income" doesn't correspond to its own output. At the same time, bureaucrats generally can't keep the savings if they prune their budgets of unnecessary expenses, and hence they don't mind overpaying. Indeed, this is a time-honored way for those who handle the public purse strings to curry favor with special-interest groups and ensure plush consulting jobs after leaving the government.

When a private individual spends $1,000 on something, it is evidence that economic value has been produced. Why? Because he could have spent that $1,000 on a wide variety of competing products—or put it to competing uses (like investing it or donating it to charity). In contrast, when the government spends $1 million or even $1 billion on a project, there is no prima facie reason to believe the activity being funded is useful to anyone. Chances are, it actually makes us poorer. This is especially true if we consider the source of the government's money: hardworking taxpayers. While you and I actually have to earn our money, all the government has to do is print it and tax us.

Chapter Eleven

BREAD AND CIRCUSES: POPULAR GOVERNMENT PROGRAMS

We were in class, no doubt learning long division or something equally important, when a shocked teacher from down the hall threw open the door: "The space shuttle just exploded!" Much to the delight of her students, this particular teacher had earlier taken the trouble to acquire a television set (on a stand with wheels—Catholic grammar schools were not flush with audio/visual equipment in those days) and was allowing her class to watch the celebrated launch. This particular flight was more popular than most, because of the presence of schoolteacher Christa McAuliffe. The students' glee turned to horror when the *Challenger* suffered an explosion and then crashed on that fateful day in 1986.

The immediate reaction to the tragedy was grief, followed by a demand to know what had caused the accident. Unfortunately, the *Challenger* disaster was not simply a case of the danger associated with mankind's brave journey to the stars. No, as subsequent investigation revealed, NASA had done a terrible job of managing the risk associated with its flights, and after the fact its administrators behaved as bureaucrats typically do—they shifted the blame and failed to fix the underlying problems.

Guess what?

- NASA wastes money and lives.
- The War on Poverty hasn't reduced poverty.
- The 1980s weren't a "decade of greed."
- Social Security is neither social nor secure.

NASA: Needlessly dangerous

A popular and technically informed account of the *Challenger* disaster is contained in Nobel laureate Richard Feynman's *What Do You Care What Other People Think?* Serving on the presidential Rogers Commission, appointed by Ronald Reagan to investigate the accident, Feynman received tips from an insider who wished to remain anonymous and uncovered the role of the booster rocket's O-ring seals in the explosion. Feynman famously demonstrated the problem during a televised hearing by using clamps to dip the O-ring material in a glass of ice water, where it soon became very brittle. (There was ice on the launch pad the morning of the *Challenger* disaster.)

As Feynman argues in his minority report—which was included as an appendix to the official document only after much petitioning and revision—the entire culture of NASA encouraged such hazards. For example, the engineers were aware of particular risks that somehow got filtered out of the official reports on their way up the chain of command. (The actual engineers gave Feynman estimates of probability-of-failure for the shuttle that were hundreds of times higher than those provided by upper management.) The *Columbia* disaster in 2003 indicated that the estimates of the engineers—and of Feynman in his critical appendix—were far closer to reality.

The problems with NASA have nothing to do with the particular individuals involved; no one would suggest a conspiracy or that the agency's higher-ups were callous about the loss of human life. On the other hand, the insights of political economy tell us that the accident should not be simply chalked up to bad luck. The incentives of an agency such as NASA encourage the policies that led to the two shuttle disasters and prevent a serious revamping of its culture to avoid similar ones in the future.

The most obvious source of risk is the use of manned flights in the first place. Many observers have speculated that most manned missions could achieve their technical or scientific purposes without humans. Yet a government agency such as NASA—which must obtain its funding from Congress, which in turn is subservient to a fickle public—must maintain the glamorous image of space exploration. This is far easier to achieve by

A Giant Leap, Indeed

Ever the rogue, physicist Richard Feynman broke away from the rest of the presidential commission and tried to get to the bottom of the *Challenger* disaster. After learning that the official estimate of shuttle failure was 1 in 100,000, Feynman assembled a group of NASA engineers and one manager and asked them to write their estimates that a shuttle flight would fail due to engine trouble (disregarding other sources of failure). The engineers wrote estimates in the range of 1 in 200 to 1 in 300, while the engineer-turned-manager initially wrote only bullet-point summaries of how the estimate could be achieved. Pressed by Feynman to give him an actual number of the probability of success, the manager initially said "100 percent." When the others looked shocked, he quickly added, "Uh, minus epsilon." Pressed to define epsilon, he clarified as 1 in 100,000. He later sent Feynman documentation to back up his number, on which Feynman comments:

> [The report] said things like "The probability of mission success is necessarily very close to 1.0"—does that mean it *is* close to 1.0, or it *ought to be* close to 1.0?—and "Historically, this high degree of mission success has given rise to a difference in philosophy between unmanned and manned space flight programs; i.e., numerical probability versus engineering judgment." As far as I can tell, "engineering judgment" means they're just going to make up numbers!…The whole paper was quantifying everything. Just about every nut and bolt was in there: "The chance that a HPHTP pipe will burst is 10^{-7}." You can't estimate things like that; a probability of 1 in 10,000,000 is almost impossible to estimate. It was clear that the numbers for each part of the engine were chosen so that when you add everything together you get 1 in 100,000.[1]

A Book You're Not Supposed to Read

What Do You Care What Other People Think? by Richard Feynman; New York: W. W. Norton, 1988.

sending astronauts, especially civilian teachers such as McAuliffe, rather than beeping robots into space.

Consider the inflated estimates of the shuttle's safety by NASA's management. This too is perfectly rational behavior, given the incentives they faced. In order to receive additional funding, NASA's official reports couldn't cast the popular shuttle program as a death trap waiting to spring. So long as the managers thought the shuttle probably wouldn't have a major mishap, it would be perfectly sensible to inflate the numbers and hope for the best. To publicize every concern of every engineer would give ammunition to NASA's critics, who coveted its funds for their own pet projects.

Even after the *Challenger* disaster, the attempts to downplay or silence Feynman's critiques were perfectly understandable. No one wanted more astronauts to die, of course, but scathing reports from loose cannons like Feynman might lead the less enlightened members of Congress to scrap the shuttle program altogether. In this light, some face-saving (if somewhat inaccurate) PR might seem completely reasonable for administrators who had spent careers in the space program.

Outer space: Too big for the private sector?

Of course, the entire discussion over the fate of NASA presupposes that the federal government has a proper role in spending billions of taxpayer dollars on sending rockets and shuttles into the sky. Supporters of the space program would point to the moon landing and other notable achievements as the obvious justification for NASA's budget. After all, surely the private sector wouldn't have financed the Apollo missions, and therefore federal funding is necessary. For more down-to-earth illustrations of the same mentality, proponents of government spending point to particle accelerators, giant telescopes, massive dams, and even base-ball stadiums as projects useful for the community that are supposedly "too big" for private financing.

The absurdity of this typical view is evident once we ask whence Congress gets all these billions to lavish on supposedly crucial programs. Why, from the private sector, of course! When JFK decided that the United States should put a man on the moon, he didn't contribute to the physicists' understanding of motion through a vacuum, and he didn't enlarge the country's reserves of steel, gasoline, and other resources used in the bold undertaking. No, what happened was that the federal government redirected billions of dollars in resources from other potential uses and channeled them instead into putting a U.S. flag on the moon (and collecting some rocks).

In a famous essay titled "That Which Is Seen, and That Which Is Unseen," Frédéric Bastiat underscored the need to look beyond the obvious benefits of government spending programs. To understand if a program is sensible, we must compare the benefits with the costs. By using up scarce resources in the space program (or building a sports stadium), the government delivers tangible benefits, but also destroys unseen possibilities of the alternative products and services that those resources could have created.

Critics of capitalism think (wrongly) that the profit and loss test is arbitrary and crude. On the contrary, it provides an indispensable barometer of the consumers' preferences over how resources are deployed. For example, when people say that government needs to subsidize a stadium or bus service, because "it wouldn't be profitable for private business," what that really means is that consumers would rather spend their money on other goods and services that would be profitable. By taxing their money and spending it on the stadium, the government hasn't suddenly changed people's tastes or created resources out of thin air. No, all that's happened is that the government has overridden the voluntary choices of the public and instead forced them to spend their money on the politically favored items.

Capitalists: Just out for a buck?

Many sensible people are aware of the considerations above. However, they feel that certain things are "more important than money" and that something might be worthwhile "even if it doesn't turn a buck." The benefits, broadly construed, of a scientific experiment or of other noble enterprises might not accrue in dollars and cents, but they are nonetheless important. Consequently, according to this view, we need the government to fill the funding gap of the free market.

This argument is completely unfounded and relies on a narrow definition of "profitable." In a genuine free market, operations can survive even if they yield no directly marketable products. For example, the $10 million X Prize (awarded to Burt Rutan for his SpaceShipOne flight in 2004) was established not by dividend-seeking investors but rather by space enthusiasts (including novelists Tom Clancy and Arthur C. Clarke) who wanted to spur the development of civilian spacecraft.

Private philanthropists also support purely abstract research. For example, the Clay Mathematics Institute (CMI) has established an endowment to finance $1 million prizes for the solution of each of seven classic mathematical problems. These problems (such as proving or finding a counterexample to the famous Riemann hypothesis of prime numbers) are quite abstract; their solution would certainly not enable CMI to gain an edge on its competitors with a new product line in order to recoup their "investment." For a different example, consider the Catholic Church's support of artists and other craftsmen: did the Vatican commission Michelangelo in order to boost revenue from tithes?

The argument over "public" funding of programs isn't about materialism versus idealism. On the contrary, it is about letting citizens spend their money on whatever ventures they support, versus the politicians taking their money and spending it for them. People who insist on using politics to trump the market are people who insist on government coercion rather than individual choice.

LBJ's war on taxpayers

Perhaps the single biggest objection to unbridled capitalism is that it results in massive income inequality. Although most people—even intellectuals—now concede that pure communism doesn't work, they still hesitate to embrace its alternative. Rather, they seek a middle ground that avoids the misery of communism as well as the allegedly unconscionable excesses of capitalism. Over the course of the twentieth century, Americans increasingly looked to the federal government as the champion of the poor. The problem of poverty was viewed merely as a failure of resolve and political leadership, as epitomized in the rhetorical question, "If we can put a man on the moon, why can't we eliminate poverty?"

Although this type of question is quite familiar to Americans, it betrays a naïve view of the world. Some conservatives have rightfully ridiculed the question because it disregards the different natures of the problems involved. (Indeed, at face value the question appears to be suggesting that the government deport homeless people into space.) Yet this actually concedes too much to the proponents of federal intervention—NASA is definitely *not* a paragon of achievement. (In addition to the shuttles and earlier accidents, the scandalous problems with the billion-dollar Hubble telescope and the 1999 loss of a $125 million Mars orbiter due to confusion over metric versus English units come to mind.) In

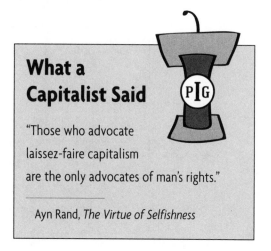

What a Capitalist Said

"Those who advocate laissez-faire capitalism are the only advocates of man's rights."

Ayn Rand, *The Virtue of Selfishness*

this respect, the comparison is, ironically, a fair one: if the federal government can waste billions of dollars and ruin lives in the space program, why can't it do the same for the poor?

Indeed it can. Since Johnson declared his war in 1964, more than $7 trillion has been spent on government anti-poverty programs, yet it's debatable whether these measures have done anything to reduce poverty. For example, from 1959 to 1964, the poverty rate fell from 22.4 to 19.0

The Decade of Greed?

Those who criticize federal anti-poverty programs are often dismissed as heartless cynics who care nothing for the poor. Yet how could any genuine advocate for the downtrodden endorse the dehumanizing Welfare State? Private philanthropy not only respects property rights, but it also treats recipients with more dignity and squanders fewer funds on overhead and fraud. When the government returns money to the taxpayers, they in turn give more to the poor. Spurred in part by Reagan's slashing of marginal tax rates in 1981, during the so-called Decade of Greed:

- Total giving grew by 56 percent in real dollars.
- Charitable giving grew at a rate 55 percent higher than in the previous twenty-five years.
- The increase in giving exceeded the increase in total outstanding consumer credit.
- Relying on correlations established between charitable giving and GDP, tax rates, and other factors during the 1955–1980 period, actual giving exceeded the "predicted" giving in every year of the 1980s, on average by $16 billion per year.[2]

percent without special oversight from the executive branch.[3] It's true (as the fan of LBJ might argue) that this steady fall in the official poverty rate accelerated somewhat during the next few years. However, this defense of Johnson overlooks the fact that the massive federal transfers didn't swing into full motion until the end of the decade. As Charles Murray explains:

> [T]he great legislative victories that required money for imple-
> mentation did not begin to affect large numbers of persons
> until about 1967–68 and did not reach full scope until the
> 1970s. The underlying principles changed earlier. The rheto-
> ric began earlier. The implementing agencies began earlier. The
> legislation began earlier. But the income maintenance and
> social action programs that were authorized during Johnson's
> legislative hegemony in 1964–66 had relatively small budgets
> and scope during his term in office.[4]

Seen in this light, one comes up with an entirely different interpreta-
tion of the War on Poverty and the Census Bureau's official poverty statistics: the poverty rate was steadily falling until the Great Society
programs fully kicked in, at which point the rate leveled off and has
remained roughly flat (or even increased during recessions) for the thirty-
five years since.

The problem isn't a lack of money, either; government handouts actually perpetuate poverty by creating a culture of dependency. As welfare
policy expert Robert Rector put it:

> The welfare system that has existed for the past thirty years
> may best be conceptualized as a system that offered each sin-
> gle mother with two children a "paycheck" of combined ben-
> efits worth an average of between $8,500 and $15,000,
> depending on the state. The mother had a contract with the

government. She would continue to receive her "paycheck" as long as she fulfilled two conditions: 1. She must not work. 2. She must not marry an employed male.

For those who argue that federal programs to aid the poor have helped minorities, Thomas Sowell responds:

> The black family, which had survived centuries of slavery and discrimination, began rapidly disintegrating in the liberal welfare state that subsidized unwed pregnancy and changed welfare from an emergency rescue to a way of life.
>
> Government social programs such as the War on Poverty were considered a way to reduce urban riots. Such programs increased sharply during the 1960s. So did urban riots. Later, during the Reagan administration, which was denounced for not promoting social programs, there were far fewer urban riots.
>
> The economic rise of blacks began decades earlier, before any of the legislation and policies that are credited with producing that rise. The continuation of the rise of blacks out of poverty did not—repeat, did not—accelerate during the 1960s.
>
> The poverty rate among black families fell from 87 percent in 1940 to 47 percent in 1960, during an era of virtually no major civil rights legislation or anti-poverty programs. It dropped another seventeen percentage points during the decade of the 1960s and one percentage point during the 1970s, but this continuation of the previous trend was neither unprecedented nor some-

---

✴ ✴ ✴ ✴ ✴ ✴ ✴

Space: The Final Frontier

If we can put a man on the moon, why can't we eliminate poverty? Good question. After all, if the federal government can waste billions of dollars and ruin lives in the space program, why can't it do the same for the poor?

---

thing to be arbitrarily attributed to the programs like the War on Poverty.

In various skilled trades, the incomes of blacks relative to whites more than doubled between 1936 and 1959—that is, before the magic 1960s decade when supposedly all progress began. The rise of blacks in professional and other high-level occupations was greater in the five years preceding the Civil Rights Act of 1964 than in the five years afterwards.[5]

Sacrosanct Social Security

One of the more unfortunate legacies of the New Deal is the third rail of American politics: Social Security. Most Americans view the era before Social Security legislation as a horrible time in which the average person was constantly vulnerable to disaster the moment an illness or accident struck, and in which most elderly people could not live out a comfortable retirement. In this benighted environment, the federal government supposedly came to the rescue, as epitomized in Social Security legislation.

As do those of other politically popular programs, the advocates of Social Security have good intentions. But they are wrong to assume that just because something is desirable the government should provide it. Yes, it would indeed be tragic if a brain clot or car crash suddenly left a woman widowed with several children and no means to support them. This is why capitalism developed life insurance policies. It would also be a shame if someone who worked diligently for forty years had to eat

Economics Made Simple

Ponzi scheme: a fraudulent investment operation paying abnormally high returns to investors out of the money paid in by subsequent investors, rather than from net revenues generated by any real business. Named for Charles Ponzi, who in 1920 promised a 50 percent return on investments—in postal reply coupons—in forty-five days or "double your money" in ninety days. Thousands of people invested about $15 million altogether, but only one-third of that money was returned to the investors before Ponzi's scheme was shut down by the federal government.

cat food upon retirement. This is why banks and mutual funds offer savings accounts and investment plans.

Even the standard argument from paternalism doesn't justify the modern Social Security system. Even if Americans will not tolerate a society in which reckless or ignorant individuals are allowed to suffer the full consequences when disaster strikes, this in no way proves the need for Social Security. Americans can and do give voluntarily to charitable organizations that specialize in helping the needy and the unfortunate. Even if one feels that government should "guarantee" accident insurance or retirement savings, there is no reason why government should administer such "guaranteed" insurance programs. After all, the government requires that all drivers have insurance in case of accident. Yet the drivers don't have to pay their premiums and mail their accident claims to the government; the auto insurance industry is still run in the private sector.

The sad truth is that the Social Security system provides an easy way for the government to borrow money. When the annual total revenues from payroll deductions exceed total payments to Social Security beneficiaries, the federal government still spends the difference, leaving a Treasury IOU in the Social Security "trust fund." Yet this gravy train will end soon in light of demographic realities. As the proportion of working to retired Americans falls, we will soon reach a point in which Social Security payroll taxes will not cover current expenditures. At that point, FDR's Ponzi scheme will come crashing down, and even leftists will (we can only hope) understand the difference between a federal transfer program and genuine savings and investment.

Chapter Twelve

RUNNING GOVERNMENT LIKE A BUSINESS

t the end of every business day, commuters cram themselves into subway cars until they are pressed together
like the proverbial sardines. Naturally, many (probably
most) passengers would rather wait for a less crowded train, but during
rush hour there will always be a sufficient number of claustrophilic riders to ensure each car is filled to physical capacity. The situation is so bad
that many frail riders, such as the elderly or those with certain medical
conditions, can't use the busiest lines at all for perhaps several hours a
day. Who or what is to blame for this disturbing feature of mass transit?
Is it the deplorable lack of compassion for one's fellow man? Is it a reflection of our society's treatment of workers as mere cattle in our dehumanizing industrial system? Perhaps racism is the culprit in the
overcrowding, as the affected riders are disproportionately black.

The problem with these suggested explanations is that they don't
account for the different outcomes between government and private services. The same inconsiderate people who cram into a subway car don't
behave that way when flying, and movie theaters stop selling tickets to a
given show once all the seats are filled. The reason is so obvious one feels
silly even stating it: private businesses want their customers to have an
enjoyable experience, and therefore don't try to pack their customers
together nostril to nostril.

Guess what?

- Waste and poor service are pre-dictable features of government ownership.

- Only .5 percent of intercity travelers use Amtrak, which lost over $1 billion in 2005.

- Rain, sleet, and snow are the least of the Post Office's problems: it has lost *millions* of parcels and borrowed *billions* of dollars.

- Government "deregulation"— like California's electricity "deregulation"— is often phony.

Such considerations, unfortunately, are beyond the bureaucrats who manage America's "public" subway systems. After all, how does it benefit the mayor of New York, or any of his subordinates, to fix this problem? It would probably cost millions of dollars to hire extra employees (and/or revamp the platforms) to enforce the new boarding limits. The extra cash would either have to come from fare hikes or general revenue; in either case, there would be huge political opposition. And for what? Is the next mayoral election really going to turn on the issue of crowded subways at rush hour?

Profits versus bureaucracy

In a neglected 1944 masterpiece, *Bureaucracy*, the great economist Ludwig von Mises explained the fundamental difference between private and government enterprises. Because private businesses are ultimately concerned with turning a profit, even large corporations can avoid the waste that so typifies government undertakings. This is because the corporation can divide its operations into smaller units and give the manager of each relatively free rein to try various approaches. This approach works because there is always an objective criterion by which to evaluate the performance: did it turn a profit, or did it lose the corporation money?

In contrast, Mises argued, a government enterprise must be managed in an entirely different way. Because its funds are obtained from the legislature, and ultimately from the involuntary tax payments of the citizens, it won't do to allow public sector managers to try various techniques as long as they're "profitable." Such a reckless policy would allow a school system to "save" millions of dollars by teaching only three months per year, or the local fire department to "raise funds" by selling all its fire engines. In the private sector there is no need to worry about such abuses, because there each firm must raise its funds from willing customers; a diner that didn't provide any forks would quickly go out of business. Yet in the government sector, where enterprises receive taxpayer money and/or monopolistic privileges, different rules apply. In the government sector, the customer isn't always right, the bureaucrats are—and bureaucrats have goals other than customer service (because the customer can't take his business elsewhere) and cost effectiveness (because the less cost-effective they are, the more money they can claim they need).

Amtrak

The story of Amtrak (whose name is a combination of "American" and "track") is typical of "quasi-governmental agencies," that is, enterprises that are nominally in the private sector but are closely controlled by the government. (Notice that this is the technical distinction between fascism, in which enterprises are state-directed, and communism, in which enterprises are state-owned.) Amtrak was created on May 1, 1971, to consolidate and bail out the failing (and heavily taxed and regulated) private rail lines that chose to participate. Although the participating railroads received common stock in Amtrak in exchange for their assets, the federal government owns all shares of preferred stock. In addition, Amtrak's board of directors is appointed by the president and must receive confirmation from the U.S. Senate.

A Book You're Not Supposed to Read

Bureaucracy by Ludwig von Mises; Grove City, PA: Libertarian Press, 1994.

From the beginning, Amtrak was plagued by Congress's conflicting goals: to both maintain intercity passenger rail service—in spite of the growing competition posed by air travel and the interstate highway system—and to become financially self-sufficient. Amtrak—surprise, surprise—has fulfilled neither of these objectives. Bowing to economic realities, Amtrak's service has been repeatedly scaled back over the years. For example, Amtrak offers no rail service to the cities of Phoenix, Las

Vegas, Nashville, Dayton, Tulsa, or Colorado Springs, even though these all have populations of over 500,000. Along with this lack of geographic availability, Amtrak fares aren't exactly for the poor: a quick price check (in February 2007) reveals that the round-trip fare from Penn Station in New York City to Union Station in Washington, D.C., runs from $134 to $346, depending on class. (The comparable fare for Peter Pan bus lines is $69, though of course the trip is longer.)

Now if a private sector rail company offered this service, it could justify the higher fare on the grounds that people preferred the speed and comfort of a train ride to a bus trip, and were happy to pay for it, as proven by the company's profitability. Similarly, it would be perfectly acceptable for a private company to restrict service to those routes that turn a profit.

But therein lines the difference between Amtrak and any business in the private sector. Amtrak can't defend its service cutbacks and high rates by appealing to economic efficiency, since it has lost money every single year of its history.[1] In 2005 Amtrak received a whopping $1.2 billion from the federal government to help make ends meet. It loses money in every conceivable way—on ticket sales and even on its food and beverage concessions. On one of its worst lines, the Sunset Limited connecting Los Angeles and Orlando, Amtrak lost $433 per passenger. Your tax dollars would have been saved if the line had been scrapped and Amtrak's customers given plane tickets instead.

Despite its abysmal record and failure to even provide "universal" access, Amtrak will probably continue to limp along. After all, as *Reason*'s Mike Lynch points out, Amtrak's busy Northeast lines shuttle many a congressional staffer and bureaucrat between home and work; the political class will no doubt continue to believe Amtrak is "worth it," as its own members enjoy the benefits, while the taxpayers (many of whom won't ever set foot on an Amtrak train) shoulder the burdens. And as for the prospects of "reform" at Amtrak: why bother getting your fiscal house in order when Congress gives you a billion-dollar margin for error?

Talk about a Toilet! New York City Subways

Say what you will about Amtrak—at least the trains are clean. In contrast, as anyone can attest from personal observation, the fully "public" subway system in New York City is often a source of relief, quite literally, for many of New York's homeless (and even for desperate late-night bar hoppers). The reason people take such liberties is because, first, the subway trains, and even most of the stations, lack restrooms, and the few functional ones are indescribable. Second, because of the perverse incentives of government control, no bureaucrat gains anything from maintaining a clean subway system. If the subway were private property, and its system run for a profit, you can bet that the company would be looking to provide a service and an environment that attracted customers and maintained its value.

Going postal over poor service

In contrast to Amtrak, the United States Postal Service (USPS) is not a corporation but a formal agency of the executive branch of the federal government. With some 700,000 employees, the USPS is the third largest employer in the U.S. (after the Department of Defense and Wal-Mart). Along with the Department of Motor Vehicles, the USPS is the butt of jokes and has a reputation for inefficiency, long lines, and uncaring bureaucrats.

The examples are legion. In the 1990s inspectors in south Maryland found 2.3 million pieces of bulk mail and 800,000 pieces of first class mail resting in tractor trailers. Because the postal service records mail as "delayed" only if it is held in the mail processing building, the tractor trailers were used so the delays would never turn up in official statistics. In 1994, in Chicago, 5.9 million pieces of forwarded mail were delayed for a month, a hundred bags of months-old mail were found in a postal truck, and 200 pounds of burned mail were discovered under a viaduct![2]

Unlike in the private sector, when it comes to the Post Office, you don't get what you pay for. Despite its poor performance, the USPS continues to hike rates. In 1981 the price of a first class stamp was 18 cents; in 2007 it is 39 cents, an average compounded increase of roughly 3.1 percent per year. After adjusting for inflation, this represents a hike of roughly 15 percent in the real price of stamps over the last twenty-five years. In exchange for higher prices, the USPS hasn't provided much improvement in the actual service. In contrast, in competitive markets innovation is the rule. For example, look at how much computers and automobiles have improved since 1981. Not only does the increase in quality offset the nominal rise in prices for these items, but if we measured the improvements in quality—say, the price of a kilobyte of memory in a computer—we'd find dramatic savings. For example, you would have paid about $47 per kilobyte of memory in your computer in 1981. Today, you'd pay a tiny fraction of a penny.

But at least the Post Office is self-sufficient!

Advocates often argue that, whatever its flaws, the Post Office isn't a burden on taxpayers, because receipts from stamp sales and other items cover expenses. The actual situation, however, is a bit more complicated. Between 1985 and 1994, for example, the federal government had total outlays (both on and off budget) to the USPS of more than $14 billion.[3] Some of these funds were earmarked to compensate for mandated rate privileges enjoyed by members of Congress, but one suspects that at least some of the $14 billion wasn't just for stamps. In addition, the government guarantees the Post Office's unfunded pension liabilities, and often covers its frequent losses (more than $1 billion in 2000) with low interest rate loans from the U.S. Treasury.[4] (In fairness, we should point out that, although the USPS owed the government $11 billion in 2002, this debt was paid off by 2005. The point remains, however, that the taxpayers certainly provide financial support to the system.)

But the biggest problem with the self-sufficiency argument is that the Post Office enjoys a monopoly. It is illegal for anyone else to deliver first class mail in the United States (although "extremely urgent" letters can be delivered as long as the private carrier charges either nothing or at least $3 for the service), and rival carriers are prohibited from depositing items in boxes marked U.S. MAIL. In every area where competition is allowed, private carriers such as UPS and FedEx dominate the market—even though these firms are subject to federal taxation while the USPS is exempt. In this light, the self-sufficiency argument falls apart.

A Book You're Not Supposed to Read

Street Smart: Competition, Entrepreneurship, and the Future of Roads, ed. Gabriel Roth; New Brunswick, NJ: Transaction, 2006.

In the nineteenth century, libertarian essayist Lysander Spooner challenged the Post Office's monopoly by launching a competing service. His competition forced the USPS to cut its rates before the government shut him down and prosecuted him. Spooner had early success in the courts, claiming that the Constitution's designation that Congress shall have the power to "establish post-offices and post roads" didn't prevent others from delivering mail; Congress ultimately ended the dispute by legislating the monopoly.

But if the government would only allow competition, the market for first class mail would be brimming with cost-cutting innovations.

Public utilities

Every summer, ice cream, hot dog, and beer vendors in big cities eagerly await the prospect of selling more of their products to customers. But they're in business for profit; government-managed utilities aren't. So every summer, the water utilities urge their customers to let the car stay dirty and the grass dry out, and electricity utilities impose "rolling black-outs" to prevent a total collapse of the power grid.

The problem is that the so-called "public" utilities charge below-market prices and enjoy a monopoly on basic service. The artificially low prices encourage waste—despite moral appeals for conservation—and because of the monopolies, alternative providers don't rush in to fill the shortages. Ironically, it is the most essential services that are reserved for shoddy government provision, while nonessentials, like steaks and plasma-screen TVs, are always available for purchase.

But didn't they try deregulating electricity in California?

Critics of the government monopoly on electricity are often confronted with a statist trump card: according to the typical story, California unleashed market forces in the late 1990s, and the result was massive disruptions in service, huge price hikes, and ultimately billions of dollars in taxpayer bailouts.

But that gets the basic facts wrong. The California episode would be better described as *re*regulation rather than deregulation, because although price controls and barriers to entry were relaxed for the generation of electricity, complicated new procedures (setting prices and guaranteeing access to network facilities) were imposed on the distribution side of the market. The result was entirely predictable to any student of economics. If consumers have legal price caps while the wholesalers must pay whatever the market will bear, in times of high demand some of the wholesalers will shut down and supply will dry up. As opposed to the California episode, the more uniform deregulation of the airline industry in the 1970s and of the telecommunications industry in the 1990s led to huge price reductions and more choices for consumers.

Government in a jam

Here's a quick experiment: Compare the quality of paved surfaces controlled by government and those controlled by private businesses. Which ones have more potholes and are closed more often and at inconvenient times?

Although government control of roads is taken for granted, economists have long debated the merits of privatization. The most obvious benefit would be the overnight disappearance of that bane of mechanized society, the traffic jam. Traffic jams are just an example of shortages, caused as always by below-market prices. For example, if New York City sold its major bridges and tunnels to private firms, it is undeniably true that the tolls for passage would rise, perhaps sharply. But one immediate implication of the supposedly unconscionable "charging whatever the market will bear" is that hundreds of thousands of productive doctors, brokers, engineers, and other workers would no longer be tied up for hours each day making the relatively short commute into Manhattan. And if the privatization reform were sweeping enough, the high profits would spur new entrants to build more bridges and tunnels and to design novel solutions that no one today has even dreamt of to ease congestion—while making roads safer and more convenient.

Chapter Thirteen

TRUSTING THE FEDS ON ANTITRUST

ome people are truly frightened by the prospect of pure capitalism. Were it not for the wise intervention of antitrust authorities, wouldn't continual mergers result in mammoth corporations answerable to no one? Free market economists like to talk about the wonderful benefits of competition, but doesn't capitalism spawn monopolies if left to its own devices? Rather than showering choices and low prices on consumers, wouldn't entrepreneurs like Bill Gates and Sam Walton take over the world and charge whatever they wanted?

As with the many other myths exploded in this book, these fears are similarly without basis. Both theory and history support the claim that free market capitalism leads to better products and services, at lower prices, for consumers. Government intervention, on the other hand, truly provides "restraints on trade."

The myth of the robber barons

In an absolutely delightful book, *The Myth of the Robber Barons*, historian Burt Folsom debunks the standard textbook treatment of the so-called "robber barons," those great captains of industry who supposedly

Guess what?

- The "robber barons" cut costs and prices.
- Free market mergers promote efficiency— government monopolies don't.
- Antitrust suits are usually filed by firms that lose in free competition.

ran rampant over the common folk before being reined in through antitrust legislation and other measures. But Folsom documents that famous entrepreneurs like Charles Schwab and John Rockefeller achieved their dominance through cutting costs and pleasing customers—just as all successful capitalists do. For example, Cornelius Vanderbilt first achieved notoriety when he (illegally) challenged the monopoly on New York State steamboat traffic that the government had granted to Robert Fulton. According to Folsom:

> Vanderbilt was a classic market entrepreneur, and he was intrigued by the challenge of breaking the Fulton monopoly. On the mast of [his employer] Gibbons's ship Vanderbilt hoisted a flag that read "New Jersey must be free." For sixty days in 1817, Vanderbilt defied capture as he raced passengers cheaply from Elizabeth, New Jersey, to New York City. He became a popular figure on the Atlantic as he lowered the fares and eluded the law. Finally, in 1824, in the landmark case of *Gibbons* v. *Ogden*, the Supreme Court struck down the Fulton monopoly.... A jubilant Vanderbilt was greeted in New Brunswick, New Jersey, by cannon salutes fired by "citizens desirous of testifying in a public manner their good will." Ecstatic New Yorkers immediately launched two steamboats named for [Chief Justice] John Marshall. On the Ohio River, steamboat traffic doubled in the first year after *Gibbons* v. *Ogden* and quadrupled after the second year.[1]

As the Vanderbilt story illustrates, true monopolists must rely on government privilege. In a genuine free market, producers cannot compel customers to purchase their products, or prevent others from competing. Ironically, the very factor needed to make a harmful and effective "conspiracy in restraint of trade" (as the antitrust laws call it) is also the factor that makes the conspiracy legal. Ask James Pennington, who sued the United Mine Workers labor union. The union had colluded with the largest coal mine companies in the country and the White House to push a new regulation that drove smaller miners like Pennington out of business. The Supreme Court ruled that if you have the government on your side, your conspiracies are fine. Antitrust lawyers know this as the Noerr-Pennington doctrine.

Under pure capitalism, a producer can "control" a market only if he provides a better product at a lower cost—surely a beneficial arrangement for a consumer. Such a producer must constantly improve quality and watch expenses lest outsiders enter the market and steal customers away. In contrast, producers who turn to the government for special privileges (either outright grants of monopoly or regulations and tariffs that disproportionately hurt their rivals) have no incentive for efficiency or customer service.

Folsom provides dozens of anecdotes illuminating the competitive edge of men who are now household names. For example, he relates a tale in which Charles Schwab describes his visit to an unproductive steel mill under his control. After explaining that the mill's manager had unsuccessfully tried various techniques to improve output, Schwab says:

> It was near the end of the day; in a few minutes the night force would come on duty. I turned to a workman who was standing beside one of the red-mouthed furnaces and asked him for a piece of chalk.
>
> "How many heats has your shift made today?" I queried.
> "Six," he replied.
>
> I chalked a big "6" on the floor, and then passed along without another word. When the night shift came in they saw the "6" and asked about it.

"The big boss was in here today," said the day men. "He asked us how many heats we had made, and we told him six. He chalked it down."

The next morning I passed through the same mill. I saw that the "6" had been rubbed out and a big "7" written instead. The night shift had announced itself. That night I went back. The "7" had been erased, and a "10" swaggered in its place. The day force recognized no superiors. Thus a fine competition was started, and it went on until this mill, formerly the poorest producer, was turning out more than any other mill in the plant.[2]

The infamous case of Standard Oil

The textbook example of a behemoth private organization that allegedly needed to be dissolved with antitrust enforcement is John D. Rockefeller's Standard Oil. Now when it comes to Rockefeller, even the critics can't complain about what he did with his fortune: by the time he died, Rockefeller had donated $550 million (and this was back when half a billion dollars really meant something). Rockefeller's money funded scientists "who found cures for yellow fever, meningitis, and hookworm,"[3] and his donations to educational institutions are well known.

In addition to his philanthropy, by all accounts Rockefeller was generous in his personality as well. According to one of his oil buyers, "I have never heard of his [Rockefeller's] equal in getting together a lot of the very best men in one team and inspiring each man to do his best for the enterprise." John Archbold, who would later become a vice president of Standard Oil, said, "You ask me what makes Rockefeller the unquestioned leader in our group. Well, it is simple. . . . Rockefeller always sees a little further ahead than any of us—and then he sees around the corner." Biographers could not find anyone—even business rivals—who could remember an instance when Rockefeller lost his temper. A serious Christian, Rockefeller once demonstrated his humility when a new accountant moved into a room holding an exercise machine. Not realizing what his new boss looked like, the accountant saw Rockefeller and ordered him to remove the machine. Rockefeller simply obeyed, and took no punitive actions against the employee.[4] This is hardly the type of "ruthless" man one would expect to be heading the gigantic Standard Oil.

A Book You're Not Supposed to Read

The Myth of the Robber Barons by Burton Folsom; Washington, DC: Young America's Foundation, 2003.

Ironically, not only were Rockefeller's private life and personality uplifting and decent, so also were his business moves. As he explained to one of his business partners, in his view they were "refining oil for the poor man and he must have it cheap and good." Rockefeller certainly lived up to this goal. After twenty years in the refinery business, Standard Oil captured 90 percent of the market—but it achieved this dominance by driving the price of kerosene down from 58 cents to 8 cents per gallon.[5]

Naturally Standard Oil outcompeted its rivals because it had lower costs. Rockefeller achieved this through various means, including the production of his own oil barrels and hiring chemists to develop hundreds of by-products (such as paint and varnish) from the refining process. Savings also came from rebates on shipping from railroads. As Folsom explains:

> As the largest oil refiner in America, Rockefeller was in a good position to save money for himself and for the railroad as well. He promised to ship sixty carloads of oil daily and provide all the loading and unloading services. All the railroads had to do was to ship it east. Commodore Vanderbilt of the New York

Central was delighted to give Rockefeller the largest rebate he gave any shipper for the chance to have the most regular, quick and efficient deliveries. When smaller oil men screamed about rate discrimination, Vanderbilt's spokesmen gladly promised the same rebate to anyone else who would give him the same volume of business. Since no other refiner was as efficient as Rockefeller, no one else got Standard Oil's discount.[6]

To many (especially its competitors), Standard Oil's rebates seem unfair. But as Vanderbilt himself explained, it wasn't a matter of favoritism. Vanderbilt too is considered a greedy "robber baron"; he didn't offer price rebates out of the goodness of his heart. As anyone who has owned his or her own business knows, bulk purchases really are more efficient and represent "real" savings; that's why businesses offer discounts on them. It's true, Rockefeller was able to leverage his advantages in production and foresight by using them to achieve lower shipping costs. But this last component of his success was no less important than his farsighted hiring of chemists and investment in better refinery equipment. Kerosene does no one any good until it is shipped to the final customer, and thus Rockefeller's efficiencies (through bulk shipping) helped poor Americans just as surely as his other innovations.

The case against antitrust

Many readers will be surprised to learn that a growing number of economists are recognizing the flaws in government antitrust enforcement, and many even recommend scrapping the operation altogether. For example, Murray Rothbard points out that forming a "trust" is really quite similar to the formation of a corporation: In the former case, many different companies pool their resources and place them under the control of a single board of directors. In the latter case, many different investors pool their

The Free Market: The Best Trust-Buster of All

One of the key charges in the antitrust suit against Microsoft was that the company unfairly used its dominance of the operating system market to "force" consumers to use its bundled web browser, Internet Explorer. (Apparently, without help from the bureaucrats hapless computer users would be unable to download and install rival browsers.) The argument had some plausibility when Internet Explorer enjoyed almost universal use.

The situation changed with the arrival of the Mozilla Firefox browser. In October 2004, Internet Explorer held 92 percent of the market. By September 2005 its share had dropped to 86 percent and by September 2006 was down to 82 percent. Firefox's, in contrast, had risen to 12.5 percent.[7]

resources and place them under the control of a single board of directors. If trusts hurt the consumer and must be banned, why not the process of incorporation too?

The conventional argument against monopolies and trusts relies on an unrealistic, static model of the economy. Yes, if all consumers had perfect information, and all producers had the same technology and costs of production, then the standard textbook diagrams showing the "deadweight loss" of "market power" might be correct. Yet this is not an accurate description of the real world. In reality, entrepreneurs have different visions, and some are better than others at delivering new products and services. It is silly to criticize a firm for controlling a large share of its market if the market exists only because of the firm's innovations. Firms do not become "dominant" by coincidence or luck; on the contrary, they have such a large influence on their respective markets because they outperformed their competitors.

The weakness of the conventional models is apparent when it comes to advertising. In the artificial world of "perfect competition" taught in introductory economics courses, advertising is counterproductive. Why waste valuable resources producing television spots that serve only to steal business from competitors? And wouldn't things be more efficient if we didn't have dozens of competing cereal brands and running shoes?

These complaints—though finding justification in the simplistic models—overlook the complexities of real life. Advertising plays an important role in informing consumers of new products or offers. Beyond this, customers *like* the ability to choose from dozens of brands. Although the critic may not see much difference between Nike and Reebok, many consumers apparently do. If seeing Michael Jordan endorse a particular shoe makes it more attractive in the eyes of young athletes, that happiness is no less real than the satisfaction derived from a shoe that is extremely comfortable.

Observations such as these—trivial as they may seem—point out the flaws in the economic models that serve to justify government antitrust action. In a free market, mergers will be profitable only when they promote efficiency, through economies of scale or some other mechanism. Absent government privileges, dominant firms are always subject to competition from newcomers. Breaking up firms that surpass an arbitrary size threshold will only introduce uncertainty and penalize success, making future innovations less likely.

A Book You're Not Supposed to Read

Antitrust Policy: The Case for Repeal by Dominick Armentano; Washington, DC: Cato Institute, 1986.

The case for Microsoft

The famous case of Microsoft highlights the many flaws in antitrust enforcement. First, we should note the historical irony: many of us can remember when anti-capitalist writers wanted the government to impose uniform standards on the emerging computing industry in the early days of the personal computer revolution. In their view, it was absurd to let competing companies produce whatever operating systems they wanted, because ignorant consumers would be helpless before so many options, and software would be incompatible with most machines. After Bill Gates solved this problem by providing an operating system and other standards that most computer users adopted, the critics changed their tune: now the government needed to step in and break up this mammoth company because its popularity gave it an unfair advantage!

The Microsoft case is also typical in that its rivals (such as IBM, Sun, and AOL Time Warner) have filed the antitrust suits. Naïve citizens might believe that disinterested regulators bring antitrust charges against large corporations, but real businessmen know the truth. As Dominick Armentano, author of *Antitrust Policy: The Case for Repeal*, explains:

> The fact is that antitrust is special-interest law. Indeed, this was the intent of the law. The antitrust laws were created precisely to be used by smaller rivals to clobber more efficient competitors. Even today, 90 percent of the cases are one firm suing another. One aspect of the Microsoft case that pleases me is that the interest-group angle has been obvious to one and all. Even the newspapers talk openly of this fact, and I think this is healthy.[8]

The very idea of the slow-moving bureaucracy trying to regulate the computer and telecommunications industries is ridiculous. For example, the Justice Department filed antitrust charges against IBM in 1969, when the firm was an undisputed giant. The case dragged on for years, with the charges eventually being dropped as "without merit" in 1982. In hindsight, it is now laughable to recall that IBM was once considered an unchallengeable force in the computer business.

The specific charges in the Microsoft case—namely that it illegally tied its browser to its operating system—show the arbitrariness of antitrust enforcement: a judge must decide if a company can "bundle" two products or must sell them separately. This is not a pure matter of legal theory or even engineering, but also one of practical business experience. By analogy, it is obvious that Ford should be able to "bundle" the engine and tires of its vehicles when selling them to customers. It would be ludicrous for a rival to complain that Ford was unfairly "tying" its tires to its successful engine and thus reducing competition in the tire business. If someone were to level such a complaint, we can imagine the baffled executives at Ford responding, "We feel it best serves our customers by providing an integrated product. But if anyone wants to remove the tires installed at the factory and replace them with others, he is perfectly free to do so." The same holds for Microsoft, with the significant difference that it is far easier to download and install a rival browser than it is to change a set of tires.

Chapter Fourteen

TRADE WARS

conomists have a bad reputation for doubletalk, and rightly so. Harry Truman famously remarked that he wanted to hire a one-armed economist, so that he wouldn't have to hear more advice with the phrase, "On the other hand...." For another illustration, there is a running joke that only in economics can two people win the Nobel Prize in the same year for theories that say the exact opposite things![1]

Despite their infamous arguments, the one thing most economists can agree on is this: when governments impose artificial barriers to international trade, they make their own citizens poorer. Indeed, the case for free trade was hammered out by theorists such as David Ricardo and rendered blindingly obvious by writers such as Frédéric Bastiat back in the eighteenth and nineteenth centuries. Nonetheless, the general public still clamors for "protectionist" measures that reduce prosperity. The layperson believes Stephen Hawking when he writes that an electron can be in two places at the same time, but scoffs in disbelief when Milton Friedman writes that free trade makes the U.S. richer. In this chapter, we'll do what we can to change this attitude.

Guess what?

- Trade makes all parties richer.
- There's nothing wrong with a trade "deficit."
- Cheap imports don't destroy jobs.
- Tariffs and other restrictions "protect" privileged workers but make other Americans poorer.

147

Tariffs are taxes on Americans

When the U.S. federal government decides to "save jobs" in Detroit by putting tariffs on Japanese auto imports, what it really does is tax U.S. consumers when they purchase a Nissan rather than a Ford. Supporters of tariffs (like labor unions) claim that the way to make the U.S. richer is to raise taxes on Americans!

Of course, the taxes on imports make them less attractive, and thus boost business for Detroit producers. This in turn allows for more, higher-paying jobs in Detroit's factories. But this only proves that tariffs help the workers in Detroit. They still make the average American poorer, because the gain in Detroit is more than offset by the loss to everyone else. To see this, suppose the government fined Americans $10 every time they ate dinner at home. Such a measure would certainly boost sales and wages in the restaurant industry. Yet does anybody think it would be a good idea for America as a whole? Would such a tax on home cooking make us all richer?

> **Economics Made Easy**
>
> **market-clearing level:** The price or quantity at which supply and demand are equal.

Protecting jobs?

The superficial appeal of protectionist measures is that they obviously raise wages in particular sectors. Tariffs on Japanese cars really do help Detroit autoworkers, and tariffs on foreign produce really do help American farmers. (If the tariffs didn't benefit any special interests, the politicians would get rid of them.) To many people, the issue then seems to boil down to choosing between the workers (who enjoy higher wages) or the consumers (who suffer higher prices). Looking at the problem in this way, people naturally side with the workers, since work is more responsible and difficult while consuming is transient and easy.

Even though it's understandable that people reason in this way, it's entirely wrong. The ultimate purpose of work is to produce something that will be used, or, in economic terms, that will be *consumed*. Without a stipulated goal, you can't even define what it means to do a "good job." If Americans suddenly lost all interest in automobiles, it would be silly for Detroit workers to continue spending most of their waking hours in factories producing additional cars. By the same token, if everyone in the world heeded the warnings and gave up cigarettes, it would be a gigantic waste if governments instituted measures to "protect jobs" in the tobacco companies. So if American consumers prefer Japanese cars, then Detroit autoworkers aren't using their labor efficiently and should switch

---

Creating Jobs for Cubans?

When it comes to international trade, leftist intellectuals suffer from a basic contradiction. On the one hand, foreign imports are supposedly bad because they put domestic laborers out of work. On the other hand, trade sanctions on Cuba are supposedly bad because they lower the Cuban people's standard of living. Regardless of one's foreign policy views, simple logic indicates that these two positions can't both be right. If levying tariffs and other restrictions on foreign imports makes the U.S. richer, then the U.S. embargo of Cuba should make the Cubans richer, and the way to create even more prosperity would be to blockade the island entirely. In the famous words of Henry George, "What protectionism teaches us is to do to ourselves in times of peace what enemies seek to do to us in time of war."

to some other occupation. In a free market where the government can't order people around, the only way for this to happen is for the workers to get laid off (or have their wages cut so much that they quit) and then seek out other employment on their own. Or, American auto companies need to do a "better job"—defined as producing cars that American consumers actually want to buy.

The popular obsession with the plight of the blue-collar worker—as opposed to the fickle consumer—is faulty for another reason: not only do tariffs hurt consumers, but they also hurt workers outside the privileged industry. For example, when the U.S. government slaps a tariff on Japanese cars, one effect is to raise the price American consumers must pay for a car. (If they buy foreign, they pay the tariff, but even if they buy American, they end up paying more because Detroit firms can charge higher prices due to the tariff.) So the tariffs would force a construction worker to pay more of his hard-earned cash for a less reliable, less gas efficient car just to shield auto workers from competition.

Classics You're Not Supposed to Read

Economic Sophisms by Frédéric Bastiat
The Wealth of Nations by Adam Smith

When the government slaps tariffs on particular products in order to protect some manufacturing jobs, this usually harms other manufacturing jobs. American car makers, for example, suffered when President Bush instituted steel tariffs. Federal sugar quotas, which make the U.S. price for sugar twice the world price, similarly drove Life Savers to move its manufacturing to Canada, where it can buy sugar from all over the world.

As these examples demonstrate, tariffs don't merely hurt consumers—they also hurt American workers. This is particularly true when we consider American export industries.

Loosely speaking, a nation pays for its imports with its exports. If Japan is to continue shipping automobiles and other products to the

United States, its people want something in return, such as Wisconsin cheese. Consequently, if the U.S. government artificially reduces how many cars Americans can buy from the Japanese, then at the same time the U.S. government (indirectly) reduces how much cheese the Japanese can buy from workers in Wisconsin.

So long as wages are free to reach their market-clearing levels, workers can always find employment. The case for free trade really isn't about jobs per se, but rather about which jobs workers should have. Yes, a tariff can artificially expand employment in the privileged industry, but only by artificially contracting employment in industries that have foreign markets. The rearrangement of workers isn't merely a wash, though: because of the government's artificial restrictions, labor is diverted away from its most efficient channels, and overall output is reduced. Although particular people can benefit from tariffs, on average tariffs make everyone poorer.

Classical wisdom

The doctrine of mercantilism claimed that the source of a country's riches was its stockpiles of precious metals. For example, the mercantilists argued that Spain grew richer when the French imported Spanish goods (in exchange for gold coins) and the Spanish, in turn, bought nothing from France. Such a trend would allow the Spanish to accumulate more and more gold coins, and this presumably demonstrated their increased prosperity.

The classical economists annihilated the mercantilist system. David Hume pointed out that the mercantilist program was self-defeating. For example, as Spain accumulated gold coins, Spanish prices (in gold) would rise, while French prices would fall. Eventually, it would be impossible to prevent Spanish consumers from buying the cheaper French goods and thus sending gold coins out of Spain. In his celebrated treatise, Adam Smith observed that the true measure of a country's riches wasn't its stockpile of coins, but rather the amount of commodities its citizens could enjoy. In a particularly famous passage, Smith wrote:

> It is the maxim of every prudent master of a family, never to attempt to make at home what it will cost him more to make than to buy.... What is prudence in the conduct of every private family, can scarce be folly in that of a great kingdom. If a foreign country can supply us with a commodity cheaper than we ourselves can make it, better buy it of them with some part of the produce of our own industry, employed in a way in which we have some advantage.[2]

The classical case for free trade was solidified in the writings of David Ricardo. Earlier thinkers such as Smith had typically argued that it would be silly, for example, for English workers to make wine if French workers could make more bottles per man-year of labor. (In economics jargon, Smith's argument said that countries should specialize in those industries in which their workers held the absolute advantage.) But Ricardo took the case further. Even if the workers in one country were better in all industries—in the sense that they could churn out more units per hour, regardless of the specific product—the superior country would still benefit by trading with less developed countries. (Economists describe this as workers specializing in the field where they hold the comparative advantage.)

In everyday life, these principles are so obvious that even labor unions wouldn't deny them. It would be silly if experienced tailors insisted on growing their own food while

Economics Made Easy

comparative advantage: a situation in which a country is the lowest-cost producer of a good, when costs are measured by the amount of alternative goods that could have been produced with the same resources. A country may be at an absolute disadvantage and still be the most efficient producer, i.e. it could have the comparative (or relative) advantage.

farmers insisted on sewing their own clothes in order to "create employment opportunities" for themselves. Instead of this reliance on self-sufficiency, in the real world it is obviously much more efficient for people to specialize in the occupations at which they are the most productive, and to trade with others who can produce other items more cheaply. This is true even for extraordinary individuals who excel in many areas. For

Economics Made Easy

absolute advantage: a situation in which a country is the lowest-cost producer of a good, when costs are measured by the amount of resources necessary to make the good.

example, a lawyer will still benefit from hiring a secretary even if he is a better typist; by hiring the secretary, the lawyer frees up his time to focus on those areas in which he really excels—those areas in which he has a comparative (not just an absolute) advantage. For a different example, a brain surgeon still benefits from the option of going out for lunch even if he happens to be a faster cook than the teenagers working at Taco Bell.

The classical economists demonstrated that international trade raises standards of living in all participating countries by deploying workers in areas where their labor is the most productive. If a particular occupation needs government regulations in order to survive, that tells us that the workers in this occupation would be more useful somewhere else. "Creating jobs" isn't the issue—creating the right jobs is what truly counts.

Debunking the deficit

Though the classical thinkers destroyed the intellectual foundation of mercantilism, it nevertheless remains an immensely popular and influential doctrine. Today's media obsession with the "trade deficit" is an excellent example. The nation experiences a trade deficit when the market value of its total export of goods (and sometimes services, depending on the method used) is lower than the market value of total imports. As with the mercantilists of centuries past, the current hand-wringing over the trade deficit suggests that our country will "run out of money" if we continue to foolishly buy more from abroad than foreigners are willing to buy from American producers. The proposed remedy for this intolerable state of affairs is the obvious one for foes of capitalism: the U.S. federal government should interfere with the voluntary spending decisions of American consumers in order to lower the trade deficit.

Free market economists have spilled much ink and crafted dozens of different arguments and analogies to illustrate the silliness of this popu-

The Beauty of Bastiat: Cheap (Solar) Imports Don't Destroy Jobs

The French thinker Frédéric Bastiat (1801–1850) was one of the most eloquent champions of free trade. His famous "Petition of the Candlemakers" is arguably the best economics essay ever written. In this brilliant satire, Bastiat urges his government to pass a law "requiring the closing of all windows, dormers, skylights, inside and outside shutters, curtains, casements, bull's-eyes, deadlights, and blinds—in short, all openings, holes, chinks, and fissures through which the light of the sun is wont to enter houses, to the detriment of the fair industries with which, we are proud to say, we have endowed the country, a country that cannot, without betraying ingratitude, abandon us today to so unequal a combat." If only the legislators would outlaw the merciless competition from the sun, then the candlemakers could expand their businesses, hire more workers, and shower untold benefits on the economy of France. Bastiat's point is that tariff supporters make arguments very much like this—and deserve equal ridicule.

lar viewpoint. One approach is to change the argument to intranational trade: if statisticians find that New Yorkers buy more goods from Floridians than vice versa, should the governor of New York take immediate action to prevent the impoverishment of his state? If this approach fails to convince the skeptic, we can push it even further: Every year, a certain physician runs a trade deficit with all the restaurants in his area. That is, the physician spends more money at the restaurants than the restaurants spend buying the services he has for sale. Does this mean the physician is slowly having his wealth sucked away by the restaurants, and that he must alter his lifestyle immediately to avert catastrophe?

Of course the answer is no; the physician's deficit with the restaurants is covered by his trade "surplus" with the hospital that employs him— that is, he spends less money on the hospital's services than it spends on his. In the same way, the U.S. trade deficit with countries such as China and Japan is (partially) offset by its trade surplus with places such as Hong Kong and Australia. International trade is more efficient when each country's workers specialize in the areas in which they have the greatest advantage. Because of this, it should not shock or worry us when (in the aggregate) Americans buy more from a particular country, and when other countries buy more from Americans. To take measures equalizing trade between each pair of countries would be as suicidal as insisting that individual people maintain trade "balances" with each other.

Admittedly, the real world is more complicated than these arguments suggest. As sophisticated critics would point out, although the U.S. has a trade deficit with some countries and a trade surplus with others, its *total* balance is in deficit; that is, Americans spend more money on purchases from the rest of the world than the rest of the world spends on American products. Nonetheless, this is no cause for alarm, and reverting to the case of individuals makes this crystal clear: even if a man runs an aggregate trade deficit with everyone else in the world, we have no reason to criticize his conduct. For example, perhaps the man is in medical or law school, and is currently using student loans to finance his meals and rent. There is nothing foolish or shortsighted about this. Or perhaps the man is retired and is selling off portions of his stock portfolio to enjoy vacations in the Caribbean. Again, outsiders have no business griping about such choices. Finally, perhaps the man is starting a new company and issues shares of stock in order to finance the new buildings and machinery that his firm will require. Here too, his aggregate "trade deficit" with respect to others is completely benign.

The trade deficit for a country is simply the summation of the trade deficits of each individual within the country. Just as an individual's deficit can be perfectly justifiable and sustainable, so too should there be no alarm over these figures when aggregated. Yet even if the alarmists were right, and the current trade deficits couldn't be sustained, the correct response is a giant "So what?" If foreigners really are stupid enough to send us goodies year after year without buying as many U.S. goods in exchange, why does this constitute a problem for Americans? The alleged problem will fix itself once the foreigners wake up to the ostensible "realities" of which the critics warn. It is as if a worrywart sees a boy licking an ice cream cone and exclaims, "Stop doing that! Don't you realize it will eventually melt?"

The trade deficit: Follow the money

Modern-day mercantilists focus on the trade deficit because they (falsely) believe that money is the source of prosperity. A trade "deficit" suggests that more money is flowing out of the country than in, and this apparently indicates a deteriorating economy. Most free market economists deal with this misconception by switching the argument from money and focusing instead on real output of goods and services; if they can convince their readers that Americans consume more stuff under free trade, they hope that is sufficient to make the case.

Even so, it is useful to take the mercantilist approach at face value to demonstrate its flaws. What the mercantilists overlook is that the trade balance must always balance. This is not an economic theory but an accounting truism. If Americans buy $1 trillion of merchandise from Japan while Japanese consumers purchase only $850 billion in merchandise from the U.S., what happens to the missing $150 billion? After all, the Japanese workers who make Nissans, PlayStations, and so on are paid in yen; they generally don't accept U.S. dollars as wages. If Japanese consumers don't want to spend as much on U.S. output as American consumers spend on Japanese products, then the gap must be filled elsewhere. For example, perhaps Japanese investors want to buy shares of U.S. stock, bonds, or other instruments denominated in dollars, and moreover they wish to invest $150 billion more in America than vice versa. Another (less typical) possibility is that Japanese citizens hold on to actual U.S. dollars as a store of wealth, just as they might accumulate reserves of gold and silver.

Except for foreigners who literally stockpile hoards of U.S. dollar bills, the money flowing out of the country (because of trade deficits) must somehow find its way back in. The exchange rate between the yen and the dollar adjusts until the total amounts are equal. If people offer more dollars for yen (intending to either buy Japanese goods or invest in Japanese assets) than others are willing to offer yen for dollars (in order to buy American goods and/or American assets), then currency dealers will see a shortage of yen and a glut of dollars, and will raise the dollar-price of yen. This depreciation of the dollar will make Japanese products and assets relatively more expensive, and American products and assets relatively cheaper. The exchange rate will adjust until people offering dollars for yen are exactly counterbalanced by those offering yen for dollars.

There is no reason for the merchandise deficit to balance, but the overall balance of trade is always in balance.

This truism highlights yet another inconsistency in the popular views of international trade. Most citizens would probably say that a trade deficit is bad while a net inflow of capital is good. Yet the two are flip sides of the same coin: disregarding actual hoarding of cash by foreigners, the only way Americans can enjoy a net inflow of capital funds is to have a trade deficit. To insist that foreigners (a) spend more on U.S. goods than Americans spend on foreign goods and (b) invest more in U.S. assets than Americans invest in foreign assets is to demand the impossible.

Chapter Fifteen

MAKING MONEY
IN THE GLOBAL VILLAGE

espite the theoretical and empirical case for free trade, those suspicious of commerce are always inventing new twists in the argument. Nowadays only the most economically illiterate clamor for "protective" tariffs and other restrictions on international trade in goods. It is fashionable instead to attack international movements of labor and capital, especially when conducted by the dreaded multinational corporations. What unites these new critics of trade is their fear and hatred of so-called "globalization."

Manufacturing a crisis

One of the most enduring myths propagated by labor unions and other trade critics is that the U.S. manufacturing sector is on the verge of extinction. According to the AFL-CIO's website, "2.8 million manufacturing jobs have been lost since the Bush [sic] took office, many of them because corporations have shipped them to countries such as China, which is creating a booming manufacturing industry on the backs of its poorly-paid workers."[1]

Even if the claims about the alleged crisis in manufacturing were true, the ultimate response is a big "So what?" There is nothing sacrosanct

Guess what?

- 🏠 Outsourcing makes the U.S. richer.
- 🏠 The manufacturing sector isn't disappearing.
- 🏠 The Internet hasn't destroyed jobs.
- 🏠 The IMF and World Bank don't help poor countries.

A Book You're Not Supposed to Read

Free Trade Under Fire by Douglas A. Irwin; Princeton, NJ: Princeton University Press, 2002.

about manufacturing jobs. Surely we wouldn't expect hundreds of thousands of Americans to be involved in the assembly of automobiles in, say, the year 2050. By the same token, countries that are currently dependent on a few cash crops will—if they experience healthy growth and development—see their agricultural employment shrink over time. This is evidence of progress, not depression, as it takes fewer workers to do the old jobs, thus freeing up workers for the new tasks unimaginable in decades past.

Yet suppose we accept for argument's sake that a country ought to have a strong manufacturing sector. Even so, the real issue wouldn't be industry employment but rather manufacturing output. If we can make twice as many tanks per worker, the fact that we lay off half the workers doesn't mean we're suddenly vulnerable to invasion. Lo and behold, American manufacturing productivity (output per worker) grew annually by 4.8 percent between 2000 and 2003.[2] It's true that total manufacturing output started falling in 2001. However, this recessionary slump followed an almost decade-long boom. From 1992 to 2000, total manufacturing output rose by 55 percent, and in some sectors (such as industrial and electrical machinery) it more than doubled.[3] So when people point to the drop in manufacturing employment since, say, the 1950s, don't for one second believe that our economy is producing less stuff than it did fifty years ago.

Outsourcing destroys jobs?

As in the AFL-CIO quote above, the critics of trade are quick to blame manufacturing job losses on cheap imports and outsourcing. Yet there is little evidence that the manufacturing slump is due to either of these popular scapegoats. Ironically, to the extent that "trade" accounts for some of the job losses, it is primarily because of a drop in U.S. manufactured exports, not because of cheap imports destroying the domestic market. According to the McKinsey Quarterly:

> After 2000, as the economy fell into recession, U.S. exports fell. We estimate that more than 3.4 million manufacturing workers were producing goods for export in 2000; by 2003, this number had fallen below 2.7 million. All told, the export slump destroyed 742,000 U.S. manufacturing jobs.
>
> On the import side, though, the picture was very different. It isn't true that manufactured goods flooded into the U.S. after 2000. In fact, growth in manufactured imports was quite sluggish from 2000 to 2003. And as we will explain, this weakness in imports actually boosted manufacturing employment in 2003 by some 428,000 jobs.
>
> Overall, then, trade accounted for a net loss of no more than 314,000 jobs (a reduction of 742,000 because of weak exports and an increase of 428,000 owing to weak imports), representing only 11 percent of the total manufacturing job loss of 2.85 million. The other 2.54 million jobs disappeared because of the economy's cyclical downturn, which dampened domestic demand for manufactured goods.[4]

In other words, manufacturers have been laying off workers primarily because the recession dampened demand by American consumers, and not because American consumers switched allegiance to foreign

Economics Made Simple

globalization: According to economist Dr. Ismail Shariff, globalization is the worldwide process of homogenizing prices, products, wages, interest rates, and profits. Globalization relies on three forces for development: freedom of labor (across open borders), international trade, and rapid movements of capital and integration of financial markets.

brands. Another problem with the blame-it-on-outsourcing approach is that the numbers simply don't add up. For example, even the most pessimistic figures estimate that 406,000 jobs were outsourced in 2004.[5] Now that's a gross figure, not a net one, meaning that it doesn't subtract all the thousands of jobs that were *insourced* in 2004. (According to the Organization for International Investment, as of 2004 the state of California alone had 561,000 jobs provided by U.S. subsidiaries of foreign companies, and 24 percent of these "insourced jobs" were in manufacturing. These new jobs weren't all created in one year, but they show that outsourcing is a two-way street.[6]) However one wants to juggle the figures, there's no way that net outsourcing can explain the huge loss of jobs in manufacturing.

Although challenging the outsourcing numbers is important—especially when one can paint just about any picture, optimistic or terrifying, with well-chosen statistics—there is a danger that such quibbling will concede too much to the critics. The market economy is a dynamic order. It is misleading to look at "jobs lost" due to some factor or other and ignore the jobs created by the same underlying processes. For example, surely more than 100 million U.S. jobs were destroyed by machinery during the twentieth century, in the sense that one could count up every single job that was eradicated by the introduction of a particular labor-saving device. But this doesn't mean that the vast majority of Americans are now unable to find work, and that those who do must sell their labor for pennies an hour. Yet arguments comparable to this lie behind much of the anti-globalization hysteria.

Outsourcing makes America richer

So is outsourcing harmless? Actually, it's better than that: it makes our economy more efficient and makes America richer.

Consider the typical case that so worries the anti-globalization crowd. Imagine a U.S. corporation that sells manufactured goods, perhaps TV sets, to American consumers. Initially the TVs are made in the U.S. by American workers, who each earn $50,000 a year. However, due to falling shipping costs and favorable trade pacts, the corporation finds it can reduce its overall expenses by closing down its U.S. plants, opening factories in China, hiring Chinese workers for much lower wages, and then shipping the TVs overseas to sell in the American market.

A Book You're Not Supposed to Read

Equality, the Third World, and Economic Delusion by P.T. Bauer; Cambridge, MA: Harvard University Press, 1983.

In this hypothetical scenario, the laid-off U.S. workers are obviously hurt, at least in the short run. They will have to take jobs that pay less (or are inferior in some other respect) to their old jobs at the TV factory. However, their loss is more than counterbalanced by the gain of the shareholders of the corporation, who are American. How do we know that the winners win more than the losers lose?

The argument is a bit subtle, but is worth the mental strain because it is crucial to understanding the efficiency of outsourcing. We know the corporation must gain more than the laid-off workers lose by the following considerations. If the proposition weren't true—in other words, if the displaced workers lost more in wages by switching to a different job than the corporation saved in production costs—then the corporation wouldn't have outsourced the jobs in the first place. It would have been more profitable to simply cut the wages of the U.S. workers while keeping the operation in America. Yet this isn't what happened (in our hypothetical worst-case scenario). So outsourcing saves the company more money than its workers forfeit.

This is admittedly a politically incorrect argument. Few talking heads on CNBC would have the nerve to defend outsourcing on the grounds that stockholders can now receive a boost in dividends that exceeds the aggregate wage reduction for working-class families. But even if this were the whole story (which it isn't), we still would have proven what we set out to demonstrate: even a hypothetical outsourcing scenario rigged to be the "worst" possible nonetheless makes Americans richer on net. If they were honest, critics of outsourcing would have to admit that their proposals would make some workers richer but would hurt other Americans even more. Such a candid admission would also play poorly on the talk shows.

A Book You're Not Supposed to Read

In Defense of Global Capitalism by Johan Norberg; Washington, DC: Cato Institute, 2003.

The foes of outsourcing always portray their stance as good for workers and "America" in general—as if rich Americans aren't part of America.

In any event, one doesn't have to choose between rich stockholders and hardworking laborers. For one thing, cutting production costs doesn't merely help Donald Trump. Virtually all working Americans have their retirement savings invested in stocks and bonds (perhaps held by an intermediary mutual fund or insurance company). When a company raises profits by shipping jobs overseas, some of the beneficiaries are schoolteachers whose pension funds can now earn higher returns.

However, the most obvious beneficiary of outsourcing is the U.S. consumer. The spike in profits enjoyed by our hypothetical TV manufacturer would be short-lived as long as it faces competition. Just as the corporation in question could outsource production and thus cut costs, so too can its rivals. The lower costs would ultimately lead to lower TV prices for American consumers, so that the gain to the corporation—which we know is larger than the loss to the displaced workers—would soon be distributed to the consumers. The corporation's profits would return to their normal level, while TV sets would be more affordable.

A dispassionate analysis reveals that outsourcing showers more benefits than the losses it imposes on particular groups. In this respect, it is no different from the development of a new machine that "takes the jobs" of factory workers. Although the affected workers are hurt by an innovation in their particular trade, obviously all workers (in their capacity as consumers) benefit from labor-saving machinery in general. The same is true of outsourcing: a worker who loses his job to China will resent the lower paycheck at his new job, but this paycheck goes further at the store because other workers have similarly lost their jobs to cheaper foreign labor. In a dynamic economy no one is guaranteed a particular job, but in the free market people are guaranteed the most efficient deployment of labor, which raises the standard of living for everyone.

The high-tech sector: Another phony crisis

Critics of globalization have a standard response to the "naïve" optimism that it is more efficient to have low-wage foreigners produce cars and other manufactured goods, while highly skilled U.S. workers concentrate on things such as software and biotechnology (just as Third World countries hope to shift their economies from agriculture to manufacturing).

In the new world economy, they claim, cheap but highly trained foreign workers are destroying even the high-tech jobs. For example, Paul Craig Roberts—former assistant treasury secretary under Ronald Reagan and now one of the most vocal critics of the Bush administration—goes so far as to claim that not a single U.S. export industry is experiencing job growth, and that this is due to free trade and outsourcing. Roberts has written repeatedly that it is not merely blue-collar jobs that are being "shipped overseas" but high-tech ones as well.

Yet if we look at the data we see some problems with this claim. According to the Bureau of Labor Statistics (BLS), total employment in "software applications" grew from 287,600 in 1999 to 425,890 in 2004, with mean wages rising as well. Contrary to Roberts's pessimism, it seems as if this high-tech exporting industry perfectly fits the pattern described by the pro-globalization economists.

These numbers may surprise you, for there are all sorts of doom-and-gloom reports on the software industry. For example, a popular report by the Economic Policy Institute (EPI) claims that between 2000 and 2004, "software jobs" were down by more than 100,000. Now, there are two interesting things here: first, one of the cited sources is the BLS itself—so even if one questions the government-collected data, that can't explain away the numbers for the EPI study. Second, if we look at the BLS figures for 2000 and 2004, it's not at all obvious which categories EPI included and which it excluded to get the figure. For example, in "Computer Software Engineers: Applications" and "Computer Software Engineers: Systems Software" (the only two categories with "software" in the title) there is a gain of 104,660 jobs in this period. Perhaps the authors of the EPI study were including other categories in their calculations? Fair enough. But if we include everything that has "computer" in its description, there is still a gain of 132,440 jobs from 2000 to 2004.

Now admittedly, there are some particular sectors in the computer industry that took a hit in this period. The point, however, is that in order to portray the entire computer (or more narrowly, software) industry as shedding jobs, one would have to pick the categories very carefully to include the ones that had losses and exclude the big gainers (at least if one wished to rely on BLS data).

There is a second problem with such pessimistic figures. Why do they all show the losses since 2000? After all, it's not as if outsourcing and "free trade" (which is in quotation marks since we don't really have free trade) turned on in 2000 and were nonexistent before then. One cynical explanation for why the alarmists go back to 2000 (rather than, say, 1999 even though the BLS has this data as well) is that the 2000 numbers capture the status of the high-tech sectors at the height of the dot-com boom. By taking a snapshot of the computer sector at its highest point, this obviously exaggerates any declines in subsequent years. Yet if we are trying to judge the effects of "globalization," it is hardly an accurate measure.

Finally, we can pose a rhetorical question to the alarmists: do they really mean to tell us, with a straight face, that the invention of the Internet (one of the main forces of globalization) has made it harder for Americans to get jobs in the computer industry?

DO IMPORTS AND OFFSHORING EXPLAIN UNEMPLOYMENT?[7]

Year	Displaced Workers Total: All Reasons	Due to Import Competition	Due to Overseas Relocation	Percentage Due to Imports and Relocation
1996	948,122	13,476	4,326	1.9
1997	947,843	12,019	10,439	2.4
1998	991,245	18,473	8,797	2.8
1999	901,451	26,234	5,683	3.5
2000	915,962	13,416	9,054	2.5
2001	1,524,832	27,946	15,693	2.9
2002	1,272,331	15,350	17,075	2.5
2003	1,216,434	23,734	13,205	3.0

Capital export is a capital idea

Paul Craig Roberts is actually one of the most sophisticated critics of the new trends in global commerce. Roberts is too smart to openly challenge the traditional case for free trade; he admits that the free flow of goods across borders makes all participants richer. However, Roberts claims that the trends of globalization change the rules of the game: when David Ricardo made his famous case for the law of comparative advantage, workers and capital equipment generally stayed put in their home countries. Nowadays, with electronic communication, smarter workers, and better legal protection in formerly backward countries, Roberts says that the old laws don't apply. Once workers and even equipment can be

A Book You're Not Supposed to Read

Creative Destruction: How Globalization Is Changing the World's Cultures by Tyler Cowen; Princeton, NJ: Princeton University Press, 2002.

shipped across borders, the Ricardian argument for free trade collapses and we can no longer be sure that trade is a win-win proposition.

The position has a superficial plausibility: after all, American workers are more productive not simply because they have a better work ethic or go to better schools. On the contrary, one of the primary reasons that U.S. workers produce more stuff per hour (and hence make higher wages) than workers in other countries is that American workers have access to better tools and equipment than, say, laborers in Bangladesh. Yet if the tools and equipment are shipped to Bangladesh, won't this lower U.S. productivity and make America poorer? Shouldn't the government therefore enact policies to keep capital inside U.S. borders?

As with most fallacies in economics, this one considers only one aspect of the situation. What the view of Roberts and others overlooks is that capital mobility enhances the productivity of the capital. By passing laws that prevent drill presses from being shipped to Bangladesh, yes, the U.S. government can (at least temporarily) prop up the wages of American workers who use those drill presses. But at the very same time, the artificial constraints reduce the earnings of the American owners of the drill presses, and moreover their losses outweigh the (temporary) benefits to the workers. On net, the government restriction makes America poorer.

We can illustrate the point with a simple fable. Suppose a wealthy industrialist, on his deathbed, is seized by horrible guilt at his massive fortune. So he tells his attorney to donate all the state-of-the-art machinery in his computer factories to randomly selected inhabitants of a small fishing community on a remote island in the Caribbean.

The attorney—well versed in the writings of Paul Craig Roberts and a frequent visitor to the website EconomyInCrisis.org—points out the flaw in his boss's well-meaning gesture: "Sir, surely you must realize that this machinery won't remain on the tropical island. If you simply hand over full control to the people picked from the island's phone book, they'll run the numbers and realize they can earn more by selling the machines on the open market than by opening factories on the island and hiring local labor. If you really want to help the islanders, you should install explosive devices on the equipment, so that if they ever get more than a mile offshore, the devices blow up the machines. This way, the recipients of the machines will have no choice but to integrate them into their local economy, where the gifts will do some good. After all, you're trying to help the poor islanders, not the multinationals that will buy the machines if we don't install the explosives!"

Obviously something is fishy with the attorney's recommendation; you don't make poor people richer by installing explosives on their gifts. The specific flaw in his reasoning is the same one committed by Roberts. He is overlooking the wealth of the capital owners—the islanders randomly chosen to receive the machines. If the industrialist follows the wacky plan to install explosives, the machines will be much less valuable to their recipients. Instead of being moved to a production plant in the U.S., Germany, or other developed economy with workers and infrastructure best suited to the machines, they'll instead be awkwardly incorporated into the relatively mismatched island factories. The financial loss of the machines' owners will more than offset the gains of the island workers.

A Book You're Not Supposed to Read

In Defense of Globalization by Jagdish Bhagwati; New York: Oxford, 2005.

Although an exaggeration, the fable illustrates an important truth about the real world: governmental restrictions on capital export destroy wealth by preventing the most efficient organization of global production. Because much of the world's capital stock is owned by Americans, U.S. citizens in particular gain from enhanced capital mobility, and U.S. citizens in particular would suffer from arbitrary controls on capital. Beyond the immediate loss would be the long-run reduction in savings and investment, because the controls would deprive investors of the freedom to use their property in the most efficient and profitable ways.

We're from the world government and we're here to help

Critics of free trade and the host of trained economists who endorse it often make an interesting argument: if free trade is so great, then how come the countries who accept money from the International Monetary Fund (IMF) and World Bank in exchange for implementing "pro-market" reforms often do worse than countries that shun the same advice and aid? Isn't this proof that apologists for capitalism are dead wrong, and that economic realities dictate a centralized, rational approach to industrial organization and protection?

A Book You're Not Supposed to Read

Why Globalization Works by Martin Wolf; New Haven: Yale University Press, 2005.

There is actually a grain of truth in these assertions. Indeed, Harvard economist Dani Rodrik has challenged the standard case for free trade by analyzing various poor countries to see whether the West's help was beneficial. (For example, Rodrik points out that Vietnam is growing faster than Mexico even though the latter has participated far more in globalization.) However, Rodrik's conclusions are faulty. The problem isn't with the textbook case for free trade, but rather with the IMF welfare program. In a typical case, what happens is something like this: the government of an "underdeveloped" country, often controlled by a corrupt military dictatorship, runs its economy into the ground while piling up massive debt. At the point of bankruptcy, the regime turns to the IMF and/or World Bank, which bail out the fledgling despots from the hole they've dug. In return for the loans or aid, the rulers agree to "neo-liberal austerity reforms" such as lower tariffs, improved budget discipline, and privatized state enterprises. Not surprisingly, the benefits of the "laissez-faire" policies never materialize, and often the countries end up defaulting on their loans and plunging deeper into stagnation.

Cases such as these don't really constitute a valid test of free trade (and more generally, the classical liberal approach to limited government). For one thing, international bureaucracies such as the IMF are hardly staffed by radical Jeffersonians, and the packages they foist on cash-strapped governments aren't derived from Bastiat. (For example, before Argentina could get its bailout, it had to agree to raise taxes because this would reduce the budget deficit.) There is also every reason to suppose that corruption infests the loan process itself. After all, the IMF and World Bank are not private entities with shareholders who could make—or lose—billions on the loans.

We also have to recognize the sampling bias of these "experiments." In order to assess the empirical success of free trade, Rodrik and other skeptics should run regressions on every country and see how much significance can be attributed to high or low trade barriers. What he has done instead is look at economies dominated by corrupt authoritarians who, as a last-ditch effort to maintain their rule, grudgingly submit to the advice of economists trained in leftist universities. This is hardly a fair test of the efficacy of market liberalism.

A better test is to look at the Fraser Institute's famous studies (available at www.freetheworld.com) that demonstrate that freedom—especially economic freedom—strongly correlates with a country's economic strength. Freedom works in practice, not just in theory.

Chapter Sixteen

THE INVESTOR CLASS: IN OTHER WORDS, YOU AND ME

In capitalism's den of rogues, no one ranks lower than the speculators and usurers. Say what you will about the predatory habits of a Bill Gates or an Andrew Carnegie, at least these tycoons provided real services (albeit at monopoly prices). In contrast, so the conventional thinking goes, capitalists who grow their fortunes simply by seizing arbitrage profits or lending their money at interest don't provide any "real" products for the public, but merely exploit the ignorance and/or desperate situation of the masses.

As we shall see in this chapter, such typical views are completely unfounded. The market incomes earned by speculators and other "middlemen" are just as deserved as those earned by brain surgeons and street sweepers. Efforts to thwart such services only make society poorer.

Interest: Sooner is better than later

It is understandable that Marxists and other similarly minded critics view interest income with particular hatred. After all, from a superficial glance it sure seems as if the capitalists live off the sweat of the working class. For example, suppose a budding entrepreneur wants to build a new factory. He borrows $10 million from investors (by issuing bonds, let us

Guess what?

- Interest income is necessary for investment.

- Middlemen, speculators, and corporate raiders benefit society.

- There's nothing hostile about a hostile takeover.

- Call options and other derivative securities make investing safer for average Americans.

suppose) and then uses the proceeds to erect the factory, hire workers, and buy raw materials. After a few months the factory is up and running, churning out radios, which are sold to retail outlets. Out of the gross receipts from these sales, the entrepreneur has to pay the wages of his workers, the continuing cost of raw materials, and the interest dividends on the bonds. That is to say, the pile of money that the entrepreneur has from selling the radios must be shared with the bondholders who haven't lifted a finger to make the radios, nor have they contributed any vital raw material, either. What's worse, the higher the interest rate, the more the capitalists "skim off the top" from the gross receipts each period. (This is why so many utopian writers of the nineteenth century dreamt of a world with a zero interest rate.)

Of course, something is missing in this analysis. After all, the entrepreneur isn't stupid. He wouldn't have agreed to the terms of the bond issue if he didn't think the arrangement would be beneficial. In essence, the bondholders provide time. The workers and suppliers of raw materials don't want to wait for the factory to be erected and the finished radios to be sold to retailers. They want to be paid immediately for their contributions to the finished product, even though those contributions won't "ripen" for some time. By advancing their saved funds, the capitalists assume the chore of waiting. Consider: the construction workers who dig a big hole in the ground on the first day of building the factory really haven't made society any better off; a big hole in the ground by itself is useless. It's only after the foundation of the factory has been laid that the contribution of the earliest workers yields fruit. By financing the project, the capitalists nonetheless allow the construction workers to get their paychecks right away, even though their services really haven't helped anyone just yet.

Loosely speaking, the interest rate is the market's measure of impatience. Rather than lending his money, a capitalist could choose to spend it on fancy cars or steak dinners in the present. The interest rate is the premium necessary to make him postpone this consumption. Looked at the other way, borrowers will be willing to pay a higher interest rate based on how urgently they want to consume in the present. In our example of the radio factory, the workers and suppliers of raw materials didn't really need the capitalist investors; they could have contributed their labor and materials for free in exchange for a cut of the final receipts from sale of the radios. But this isn't what happens in the real world, because most workers are too impatient to wait that long. They would rather be paid up front for their work, even though months or years may pass before the final product comes to market. It is the capitalist class—and this class is everyone with savings and investment accounts; that is, you and me—that makes this option possible.

The importance of middlemen

Although they may object to the prices charged, most people concede that the true producers of a good deserve to be paid. So yes, the farmer ought to earn a living from growing oranges, because oranges are good to eat and the farmer has produced them. In contrast, the hated middleman apparently produces nothing of value; he simply "buys low and sells high" and doesn't actually increase the amount of oranges (or anything else). It seems as if the middleman is nothing but a parasite.

One way to meet this typical objection is to point out its dubious metaphysics: when we think about it, the distinction between "true" producers and "mere" middlemen is quite fuzzy. After all, even the farmer doesn't create the oranges from nothing; he has to take certain ingredients (seeds, fertilizer, sunshine, etc.) and follow a certain procedure in order to get the desired product. How is this so fundamentally different from the middleman, who takes certain ingredients (oranges from the farmer, cardboard boxes, eighteen-wheelers, etc.) and follows a certain procedure to get the desired product (Florida oranges in Alaskan grocery stores)?

The hatred of middlemen overlooks the crucial fact that modern economies are far too complex to be controlled by a single mind. The "economic problem" is not simply to determine how many oranges, apples, and sneakers in size 15 should be produced at a given time. There is also the quite complicated problem of where these items should be produced and how they will be distributed to the final consumers. This latter problem is just as important as the former. It does no good for Alaskans to know that millions of juicy oranges have been harvested in

Everyone Run! It's the Currency Speculators!

To the average leftist, the only thing worse than a domestic speculator is a foreign speculator. In particular, perhaps the lowest form of life is the currency speculator who "attacks" an ailing South American currency and thereby causes inflation and stagnation in the victimized countries. In reality, what happens is this: The irresponsible government prints money like crazy in order to curry favor with the public. However, it would be embarrassing to allow the domestic currency to depreciate against other currencies, and so the government "pegs" its money at a ridiculously overpriced exchange rate. Speculators know that even governments can't overturn economic law, and so begin selling the artificially overvalued currency to the irresponsible government, which ultimately admits reality and lets the exchange rate reflect its spree with the printing press. As in other areas, here too the speculators speed the price adjustments in the market, so that these signals are as accurate as possible.

Florida unless there is some means to deliver those oranges to them. By "buying low and selling high," middlemen perform the vital service of shipping goods from the site of production to retail outlets where they are demanded by the consumers. The hated "markup" (the difference between the farmer's price for his goods and the retail price to the consumer) is proportional to the importance of his actions; the middleman makes the most profit when he ships goods from areas of relative plenty (low price) to areas of relative scarcity (high price).

Beyond actual transportation of goods, middlemen also provide more intangible services due to superior knowledge or economies of scale. For example, one way that a bank makes money is to charge a higher interest rate on its loans than it pays out to depositors. Critics view this as pure exploitation. The bank is in a position of relative power and so jacks up the rate for its own loans and refuses to pay a "fair" amount to its depositors. But in reality, the bank performs a useful role as financial intermediary—a middleman. Because of its size and personnel, the bank is in a much better position to weather the default on a loan than any individual investor would be.

This is easy to see if we pretend for a moment that there were no banks. A young couple who wanted to buy their first home would have to make arrangements with, say, 100 other couples willing to loan them money. Of course this would be very time-consuming and difficult, since most of the couples wouldn't know each other, and because all sorts of things might happen to the borrowing couple (job loss, heart attack) that would completely wipe out the savings of the others. These problems are eliminated when all parties work through a bank: the prospective home buyers deal with one institution, and the lenders have a much safer investment (as the bank pools its loans over many borrowers, any individual default isn't catastrophic). The benefits of this arrangement are not as tangible as the fruit on a farmer's field, but they are just as real, and that's why the bank can stay in business even though it charges a markup on loaned funds.

The farsighted speculator

It's easy enough to justify the actions of the geographical speculator, who buys low (oranges in Florida) and sells high (oranges in Alaska). But what of the temporal speculator, who buys low today in order to sell high in the future?

The analysis is basically the same. If a speculator thinks a certain commodity such as oil will have a much higher price in the future, it will pay for him to buy oil now (at the relatively low price), hold it off the market until the price rises, and then sell it for a profit. Ironically, this speculative behavior achieves exactly what environmentalists want—it conserves scarce resources for future generations! Just as speculators ensure that Floridians don't eat all the oranges, so too do speculators ensure that people in the present don't burn all the oil.

The suspicion of the temporal speculator is due to a misunderstanding of cause and effect. Suppose a farsighted individual forecasts a famine next year, and thus starts stockpiling wheat. As the famine nears, more and more people see it coming, and the price of wheat goes through the roof. The speculator now empties his silos and earns huge profits. Now, the critic might think that the high prices were caused by the speculator when he stockpiled the silos. Thus many people believe that speculators serve no useful purpose and merely "manipulate" the market to make a profit. But this is a bad explanation. If it really were true that speculators could make a sure profit by stockpiling a commodity (thereby driving up its price) and then unloading it, then speculators would be infinitely rich—they would just keep doing it over and over again.

In reality, the speculator (if successful) performs the exact opposite task—his actions smooth out prices over time. The speculator buys when the price is low—pushing prices up. And then he dumps the product when the price is high—pushing prices down. Notice too that the speculator does exactly what society wants him to do: when he correctly anticipates a famine before most other people, his behavior conserves the wheat during the times of plenty and stores it for the time of need.

Futures and other derivatives:
To each according to his ability...

We've seen the beneficial role played by the successful speculator in the case of physical commodities such as wheat and oil. But what about purely financial deals that (apparently) involve nothing more than pieces of paper and abstract numbers? Isn't this a zero-sum game, where the speculator wins only by forcing someone else to lose?

On the contrary, purely financial speculation performs a vital role in the market economy. Let's go back to the wheat example. In reality, our hypothetical speculator might not stockpile as much wheat as the price differences alone would suggest, for the simple reason that the person who wisely forecasts a famine need not be a person who's very knowledgeable about renting silos, dealing with farmers, and marketing wheat. Thus, even though this prescient individual may anticipate, say, a tripling in the price of wheat over the next twelve months, he might not be able to put this information to much use, if the only way to act on his hunch is to stockpile wheat.

Economics Made Simple

forward market: a market in which participants agree today to exchange commodities or other assets for money (at the "forward price") on a specified future date. No money changes hands until the contract maturity date.

Fortunately, modern economies have developed sophisticated forward and futures markets in commodities and other assets. With these

179

possibilities at his disposal, our hypothetical speculator doesn't need to worry about the practical details of acquiring and storing the wheat. Instead, he can simply buy a large number of wheat futures, which entitle the bearer to purchase a specified quantity of wheat, at some pre-specified price, on a particular date in the future. Our speculator doesn't need to physically store wheat—he just needs to hang on to his collection of wheat futures. As time passes and more people become aware of the impending famine, the current (spot) price of wheat will rise in response, which in turn will raise the value of the speculator's futures contracts. After realizing this gain, the speculator can sell the futures before their stated maturity date, and wash his hands of the whole matter without ever seeing a grain of wheat. Nonetheless, the speculator's profit still reflects his service to the community. This is because his initial purchase of the wheat futures induced others to stockpile more wheat than they otherwise would have. (For one thing, the other parties to the futures contracts would have an incentive to stockpile wheat to hedge their exposure to increases in the spot price of wheat.)

Other types of derivative securities follow similar principles. For example, a put option on a share of stock gives the holder the right (but not the obligation) to sell shares of the stock at a locked-in price (called the exercise or strike price). An individual investor might purchase put options to limit his exposure to drops in the prices of stocks held in his portfolio. The existence of put options thus allows the conservative investor to shift much of the risk of investing onto the shoulders of others who are either more knowledgeable or have a more diversified portfolio and can thus deal with the risk more effectively. In our earlier example, the wheat futures contract

Economics Made Simple

futures market: a market very similar to the forward market, but where changes in the futures price are "marked to market" every day, where the gainer's account is credited and the loser's is debited.

allowed our speculator to focus on his advantage—forecasting wheat prices—and avoid his disadvantages—buying, storing, and selling actual wheat. So too for other derivatives: they enhance the division of labor and allow people to specialize in those areas in which they excel. Far from being a meaningless shuffle of paper and bookkeeping entries, the innovative financial instruments characteristic of Western economies raise total output and the standard of living for everyone. Even people who know nothing of call or put options benefit when large companies can expand their planning horizons because derivatives give them more control over risk.

Raiders of the lost corporation

Even the infamous "corporate raider" performs an important service. Consider the character played by Danny DeVito in the film with the charged title *Other People's Money*. DeVito's character, "Larry the Liquidator," is a New York–based financier who uses his computer to identify acquisition targets. In this case, Larry implements a "hostile takeover" of a family-run wire and cable company and plans to fire all the employees and sell off the company's assets piecemeal to the highest bidder. In the process, of course, Larry will make a hefty profit but leave the small town in shambles. By casting DeVito as the ruthless Larry, and Gregory Peck as the patriarch who wants to save the company, the film's creators leave no doubt as to the hero and villain in this tale.

This all too typical depiction of corporate raiders ignores or glosses over a few inconvenient facts. First, how is it that Larry the Liquidator— a stranger from New York—can waltz into the small town and fire everyone in the company? Does he have a small army of thugs at his command? Actually, no. The reason Larry has such "power" is that he manages to convince a majority of shareholders in the company to go along with the "hostile" takeover. And even here, intimidation isn't his tactic; he merely demonstrates to them that they will make more money with his plan than under the status quo. This is proof that the company is wasting the assets at its disposal, and that the economy would be better off if the company were disbanded.

A Book You're Not Supposed to Read

The Power of Economic Thinking by Mark Skousen; Washington, DC: BNA Books, 2002.

Ultimately, the corporate raider can make money only if the total net value of the company's assets are worth more than the total price of its stock shares. For example, if the total stock shares of a company are valued at $100 million, then the value of this company as a going concern is estimated (by the market) to be roughly $100 million; that's how much someone would have to pay to buy the company outright and lay claim to any future dividends that its stock paid. Now suppose that the owner fired all the employees, sold all the inventory, sold the equipment and buildings owned by the company, and finally paid off any outstanding debts that the company owed. After doing all this, if he ended up with more than $100 million, then liquidating the company is a profitable move, and also the one most advantageous to society—it is inefficient and wasteful to lock up scarce resources in this arrangement. The tools, equipment, and factories would be more productive if they were transferred to different companies.

In the real world, things aren't so simple. Large companies aren't owned by single individuals, but often by absentee shareholders. Often it is management, not the shareholders, who really exercise control of the company, and management will tend to act in its own interests, rather than those of the shareholders. In this setting, the corporate raider—with his ability to raise large amounts of capital, perhaps by issuing "junk bonds" (bonds that pay high yields, because the investment is considered risky)—rescues powerless shareholders captive to an entrenched and bloated management.

The corporate raider earns a profit the same way all entrepreneurs do—by transferring resources to uses with higher value. When a company lays off its workers and shuts its doors, the people involved endure hardship, of course. But by the same token, the dozens or hundreds of companies that buy up the assets of the "raided" firm can thereby expand employment, benefiting the workers in those towns. And yes, it is sad that a family-run business may have to shut down after several generations. But the way to avoid this outcome is to (a) stay profitable and/or (b) keep ownership in the family, rather than raising money from outside investors. In *Other People's Money*, Gregory Peck's character wanted to take the shareholders' money when they bought into the company, but he didn't like their decision to sell later on, and he wanted the company to retain its physical assets, even when its resources could have been more productive in other enterprises. Yet for some reason he was depicted as the noble and selfless hero!

A TWELVE-STEP PLAN FOR UNDERSTANDING THE FREE MARKET

In the previous sixteen chapters we have covered a wide range of topics. Time and again we saw how misguided the typical objections to capitalism often are. In conclusion I offer the following twelve-step plan for understanding the free market:

1. Admit that government "solutions" are a problem.

2. Have faith that human beings can interact peacefully, and that economic blessings are available for all.

3. Surrender to the fact that certain social ills cannot be eradicated by force or political "will."

4. Ask yourself, "Do I want to advocate self-sufficiency and voluntary means, or do I want to look to politicians every time I don't like something?"

5. Survey the past record of governments when it comes to economic "planning" or other alleged improvements.

6. Learn to look for the hidden costs of government intervention, rather than the superficial benefits.

7. Understand the role of market prices, and why tampering with them interferes with the job they have to perform.

8. Study history. Examine whether governments that violated private property rights stayed out of their citizens' other affairs.

9. Before condemning a market outcome as unjust, first understand why it occurs.

10. Study other "spontaneous" social institutions, such as language and science, where no one is "in charge" and yet the outcome is quite orderly.

11. When politicians propose a new program, remember how much they said it would cost at the outset. Compare that number to the actual amount spent.

12. Go through the newspaper and discover how government meddling causes or exacerbates the conflict in virtually every story.

ACKNOWLEDGMENTS

My biggest debt is to Tom Woods for suggesting that I write this book, and for introducing me to the staff at Regnery. I would also like to thank Jeff Tucker of Mises.org, Lew Rockwell of LewRockwell.com, and Sheldon Richman, editor of *The Freeman*, for granting permission to use material that I first developed for their outlets. Various correspondents on the Mises e-mail discussion list provided me with numerous references and other tips that improved the book. Special thanks also to Burt Folsom, who arranged to have a copy of his *The Myth of the Robber Barons* sent to me when I realized that my own was in storage. My brother Al provided reassurance that my discussion of the Clay Mathematics Institute wasn't completely off-base. Mark Steckbeck alerted me to Irwin's *Free Trade Under Fire*, which provided one of the tables in Chapter 15. Mark Yanochik provided me with his research on slave prices and wage rates in antebellum America. Rob Bradley provided tremendous help for the discussion of energy and oil reserves. Harry Crocker was my main contact at Regnery, guiding me through the entire process, and I was helped as well by my editor, Tim Carney. Finally, I would like to thank my wife, Rachael, who not only proofread the chapter drafts but also dug up useful material, including Mary Meyer's shocking airbag research.

NOTES

Chapter One

Capitalism, Profits, and Entrepreneurs

1. Paul Samuelson and William Nordaus, *Economics* (New York: McGraw-Hill, 13th edition, 1989), 837.

2. Ludwig von Mises, *Economic Policy: Thoughts for Today and Tomorrow* (Washington, DC: Regnery, 1989), 10.

Chapter Four

The Case against Anti-discrimination Laws

1. Walter Block and Walter Williams, "Male-Female Earnings Differentials: A Critical Reappraisal," *Journal of Labor Research*, Vol. II, No. 2, 1981.

2. Thomas Sowell, *Is Reality Optional?* (Stanford: Hoover Institution Press, 1993), 158.

3. Excerpts from Walter Williams's "Repeal the Davis-Bacon Act of 1931," *Capitalism*, December 7, 2003, http://www.capmag.com/article.asp?ID=3357.

Chapter Five

Slavery: Product of Capitalism or of Government?

1. "Slavery, Profitability, and the Market Process," *Review of Austrian Economics*, Vol. 7, No. 2, 1994, 21–47.

2. Ludwig von Mises, *Human Action*, 3rd edition (Auburn, AL: Ludwig von Mises Institute, 1998), 630–31.

3. Hans-Hermann Hoppe, *Democracy: The God That Failed* (New Brunswick, NJ: Transaction Publishers, 2001), 24–25, footnote 25.

4. Thomas Sowell, *Conquests and Cultures: An International History* (New York: Basic Books, 1998), 167–68.

5. Data from Robert A. Margo and Georgia C. Villaflor, *Journal of Economic History*, Vol. 47, No. 4, 873–95.

Chapter Six

How Capitalism Will Save the Environment

1. Robert Bradley, Jr., *Energy, the Master Resource* (Dubuque, IA: Kendall/Hunt Publishing Company, 2004), 88.

2. William M. Brown, "The Outlook for Future Petroleum Supplies," in Julian Simon and Herman Kahn, eds., *The Resourceful Earth* (Malden, MA: Blackwell, 1984), 362.

Chapter Seven

Ensuring Safety: The Market or Big Brother?

1. http://www.ilr.cornell.edu/trianglefire/narrative1.html.

2. J. H. Huebert, "Free-Market Justice Is in the Cards," *The Freeman*, April 2005, 29–30.

3. http://www.wsws.org/public_html/prioriss/iwb7-1/valuje.htm.

4. Milton Friedman, *Free to Choose* (New York: Harcourt Brace Jovanovich, 1980), 206.

5. Milton Friedman, *Capitalism and Freedom* (Chicago: University of Chicago Press, 1962), 159–60.

6. Howard Husock, "Jane Jacobs, 1916–2006: New York's indispensable urban iconoclast," *City Journal*, April 27, 2006, http://www.city-journal.org/html/eon2006-04-27hh.html.

7. http://www.stat.uga.edu/~mmeyer/airbags.htm.

Chapter Eight
Settling Debts

1. U.S. Census Bureau (Statistical Abstract).

2. Ibid.

Chapter Nine
Money and Banking

1. Milton Friedman, *Money Mischief: Episodes in Monetary History* (New York: Harcourt Brace Jovanovich, 1992), 197–98.

2. http://www.usagold.com/GermanNightmare.html.

3. George Selgin and Larry White, "How Would the Invisible Hand Handle Money?" *Journal of Economic Literature*, Vol. 32, No. 4, 1994, 1718–49.

4. Ibid.

Chapter Ten
Growing Pains

1. Historical note: Before they were rendered impossible by the macroeconomic wizards, major downturns were always called "depressions." Nowadays they are "recessions." After all, the federal government is there to protect us from another free market depression, so obviously they can't occur anymore.

2. Murray Rothbard, *America's Great Depression* (Auburn, AL: Ludwig von Mises Institute, 2000), 190.

3. Ibid., 205.

4. Ibid., 213–14.

5. Ibid., 187.

6. Larry Reed, "Great Myths of the Great Depression," Mackinac Center for Public Policy, 1998.

7. Ibid.

8. Ibid.

9. Mark Skousen, *Economics on Trial: Lies, Myths, and Realities* (Scarborough, Ontario: Irwin, 1990), 39–40.

10. Ibid., 42–43.

11. Mark Skousen, *The Structure of Production* (New York: NYU Press, 2007).

Chapter Eleven

Bread and Circuses: Popular Government Programs

1. Richard Feynman, *What Do You Care What Other People Think?* (New York, W. W. Norton, 1988), 183.

2. Richard McKenzie, "Decade of Greed?" *National Review*, August 31, 1992, http://www.highbeam.com/library/docFree.asp?DOCID=1G1:12666369.

3. http://www.census.gov/hhes/www/poverty/histpov/hstpov2.html.

4. Charles Murray, *Losing Ground* (New York: Basic Books, 1984), 48.

5. Thomas Sowell, "War on Poverty Revisited," *Capitalism*, August 17, 2004, http://www.capmag.com/article/asp?ID=3864.

Chapter Twelve

Running Government Like a Business

1. As noted by Ronald Utt in "Springtime for Amtrak and America," Heritage Foundation Backgrounder Report, May 3, 2006, http://www.heritage.org/Research/Budget/bg1932.cfm.

2. Dr. Edward Hudgins, "Postal Service Privation," testimony to the Appropriations Subcommittee on Treasury, Postal Service, and General Government of the U.S. House of Representatives, April 30, 1996, http://www.heartland.org/pdf/15502.pdf.

3. Ibid.

4. Ibid; Scott Esposito, "Time for the Mail Monopoly to Go," *The Freeman*, Vol. 52, No. 2, February 2002.

Chapter Thirteen
Trusting the Feds on Antitrust

1. Burton Folsom, *The Myth of the Robber Barons*, 4th edition (Washington, DC: Young America's Foundation, 2003), 2.

2. Ibid., 63–64.

3. Ibid., 98–99.

4. Ibid., 93–94.

5. Ibid., 83.

6. Ibid., 87.

7. http://reviews.cnet.com/4520-10442_7-6656808-1.html.

8. "The Anatomy of Antitrust: An Interview with Dominick Armentano," *Austrian Economics Newsletter*, Fall 1998, Vol. 18, No. 3, available at http://www.mises.org/journals/aen/aen18_3_1.asp.

Chapter Fourteen
Trade Wars

1. Economists are not actually eligible for the original prize established by Alfred Nobel. What they *can* receive is the Bank of Sweden Prize in Economic Sciences in Memory of Alfred Nobel, established in 1969. The joke refers to the joint recipients of the prize in 1974, Friedrich Hayek (a classical liberal) and Gunnar Myrdal (a socialist).

2. Adam Smith, *Wealth of Nations*, Book IV, Chapter II.

Chapter Fifteen
Making Money in the Global Village

1. http://www.afl-cio.org/issues/jobseconomy/exportingamerica/.

2. http://www.whitehouse.gov/cea/forbes_nabe_usmanufacturing_3-26-042.pdf.

3. http://www.cato.org/testimony/ct-dg062101.html.

4. http://www.forbes.com/manufacturing/2005/11/10/trade-jobs-economy-cx_1110mckinsey.html.

5. http://www.news.cornell.edu/releases/Oct04/Bronf.outsourcing.rpt.lm.html.

6. http://www.nga.org/portal/site/nga/menuitem.9123e83a1f6786440 ddcbeeb501010a0/?vgnextoid=a90fcd59c4f48010VgnVCM1000001a01010a RCRD.

7. Douglas A. Irwin, *Free Trade Under Fire* (Princeton, NJ: Princeton University Press, 2002), 97 (in turn based on BLS data).

INDEX

discrimination (continued):
male/female wage gap and, 29,
34, 38–39; meaning of, 29, 32;
private property and, 33–34;
unions and, 29, 37
Drabble, Margaret, 106
drug approval standards, 68–71

E
eBay, 65
economic growth: government
spending and, 111–14; inflation
and, 112; statistics for, 108–11,
111–14
Economic History (Wahl), 41
Economic Policy Institute (EPI),
166
Economic Sophisms (Bastiat), 150
economics: Austrian school of, 88,
98, 99–100; growth in, 108–14;
monetarist theory of, 98–99;
Soviet, 5–7
*Economics and the Environment:
A Reconciliation* (ed. Block),
57–59
Economics in One Lesson (Hazlitt),
15, 66
*Economics on Trial: Lies, Myths,
and Realities* (Skousen), 110
EconomyInCrisis.org, 168
Ehrlich, Paul, 53–54
*Emancipating Slaves, Enslaving
Free Men* (Hummel), 46
endangered species, as commodi-
ties, 49–50
Energy: The Master Resource
(Bradley and Fulmer), 53

Engerman, Stanley L., 41
environment: capitalism and,
49–59; conservation and, 49,
50–52; endangered species and,
49–50; government intervention
and, 49; oil reserves and, 49; pollution and, 49; recycling and,
54–57; socialism and, 58–59;
Soviet Union and, 58–59
*Environmental Overkill: Whatever
Happened to Common Sense*
(Ray), 57
EPI. *See* Economic Policy Institute
*Equality, the Third World, and Eco-
nomic Delusion* (Bauer), 163
exports. *See* trade, international

F
FAA. *See* Federal Aviation Admin-
istration
Family and Medical Leave Act
(FMLA), 38–39
fascism, 129
FDA. *See* Food and Drug Adminis-
tration
*FDR's Folly: How Roosevelt and His
New Deal Prolonged the Great
Depression* (Powell), 103
Federal Aviation Administration
(FAA), 61, 67–68
Federal Aviation Agency, 67
Federal Reserve, 97, 99, 100–101
Federal Reserve Act of 1913, 100
Feynman, Richard, 116, 117, 118
fiat currency, 89, 90, 91
Finney, Tremika, 75–76
Flynn, John T., 105, 108

Truman, Harry, 147
Trump, Donald, 164

U

UL. *See* Underwriters Laboratories
The Ultimate Resource (Simon), 50
Underwriters Laboratories (UL), 63, 65
unemployment: Great Depression and, 102, 104–5; inflation and, 112; Internet and, 159, 165–67; minimum wage laws and, 17, 23–25; trade, international and, 147, 150–51
unionization, 26, 28
unions. *See* labor unions
United Mine Workers labor union, 139
U.S. Bureau of Mines, 56
U.S. Geological Survey, 56
United States Post Office (USPS), 127, 131–33
Upshaw, William, 38
USPS. *See* United States Post Office

V

ValuJet disaster (1996), 67, 68
Vanderbilt, Cornelius, 138, 141–42
Vedder, Richard, 25
The Virtue of Selfishness (Rand), 26, 121
Visa, 64

W

wages and salaries: of CEOs, 17, 19–21; male/female wage gap and, 29, 34, 38–39; minimum wage laws and, 17, 23–25; in

professional sports, 17–19; supply and demand and, 17
Wahl, Jenny, 41, 42
Wal-Mart, 65, 131
Walton, Sam, 137
War on Poverty, 115, 121–25
water-diamond paradox, 18
The Wealth of Nations (Smith), 11, 14, 22, 150
welfare, 74, 123–24
What Do You Care What Other People Think? (Feynman), 116, 118
What Has Government Done to Our Money? (Rothbard), 90
White, Larry, 94
Why Globalization Works (Wolf), 170
Wie, Michelle, 20
Williams, Serena, 20
Williams, Venus, 20
Williams, Walter, 32
Wolf, Martin, 170
Woods, Tiger, 20
Woolf, Virginia, 29–30
workers: capitalism and, 2–3; freedom to choose and, 2–3; labor unions and, 25–28; protection of, 61, 62; socialism and, 2–3; standards of living and, 22; trade, international and, 150; unions and, 4
World Bank, 159, 169–70
World Conservation Union, 50
World War II, 86, 97; Great Depression and, 106–8

Z

zoning regulations: crime and, 61, 71–73

Other Politically Incorrect Guides™

0-89526-047-6, $19.95, paperback

0-89526-013-1, $19.95, paperback

0-89526-031-X, $19.95, paperback

1-59698-003-6, $19.95, paperback

1-59698-013-3, $19.95, paperback

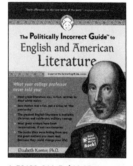

1-59698-011-7, $19.95, paperback

1-59698-500-3, $19.95, paperback

1-59698-501-1, $19.95, paperback

Regnery Publishing

created the bestselling Politically Incorrect Guide™ (P.I.G.) series to tackle a variety of hot topics in our society—issues that have been hijacked by politically correct historians, academia, and media. Inside every P.I.G. you'll find politically correct myths busted with an abundance of cold, hard facts.

REGNERY

To see our full list of guides, visit **www.Regnery.com/pig.html**
Available wherever books are sold, or call 1-888-219-4747